Ken

WRITE YOUR LIFE

A Guide to Autobiography

Wrightbooks Pty Ltd
PO Box 2301
North Brighton
Victoria 3186
Ph: (03) 596 4262
Fax: (03) 596 4206

National Library of Australia
Cataloguing-in-publication data:

Moon, Kenneth, 1928-
Write your life — a guide to autobiography.
ISBN: 0 947351 96 5.
1. Autobiography - Authorship I. Title.
808.06692

Cover design by Rob Cowpe
Printed in Australia by Australian Print Group

ISBN: 0 947351 96 5

Contents

Acknowledgements

I wish to thank my incomparable wife, virtually co-author of this work; Ken Forster, for his extended piece on Dornford Yates, and many other assistances; Shirley McLaughlin for much professional comment on the text; my painstaking and gracious editor; and finally all those authors in the too-numerous-to-mention category whose fragments of excellence in writing sprinkle these pages.

Ken Moon,

Sydney, Spring 1994

When one reaches the decline of life it is imperative to try and gather together as many as possible of the sensations which have passed through our particular organism...which without this slight effort would be lost forever. To keep a diary, or write down one's own memories at a certain age, should be a duty "State-imposed".......

PLACES OF MY INFANCY,
Guiseppe Tomasi di Lampedusa

Chapter One

Writing Your Life

.. oblivion is a stupid monster that has devoured too many generations. ...Escape oblivion. Write your own history, all of you who have understood your life and sounded your heart.

[George Sand, *Histoire de ma Vie*]

Every Life is Unique

That statement is worth repeating. Every ... life ... is ... unique. Hence, *your life is unique*. It never had, nor ever will have, a clone. And to state this with maximum flourish —*you* are the only person in the whole history of the complete universe who can write this life of yours from the inside.

Others can relate it as observers, from without; and commendably enough, too, because biography has its own unassailable legitimacy. But only the *auto*biographer can render a life as the actual experiencer. Why, though, write your life at all? People offer many reasons for attempting to commit their days to record, and we'll look at some of these reasons in more detail presently.

Generally, there is more than just some ambition to publish and collect royalty cheques; or simply to get one's personal history onto paper.

It's more likely that you have some inner compulsion. You'd like to sort out all that Past you've been accumulating: its patterns and directions. There's an urge to recreate it, feel it all again on the pulses.

... a celebration of living and an attempt to hoard its sensations. [Laurie Lee, I CAN'T STAY LONG]

It's yours, that Past; and you do not want it evanescing into oblivion forever.

This in its turn makes autobiography something of an inward journey. A bearing of the torch to the back of that cave that is *you.* So much so, that you might well not be at all clear yourself about why you have this call to write up your years ... until you've done it and then read what you've written!

Some days ago, amongst old papers, I came on an American magazine with one of my early short stories — ALWAYS GOODBYE. It told of two children who, when their father received a posting to the US, spent their last afternoon walking all their familiar paths ... saying Goodbye.

This reminded me that the first story I ever had published was about an old and solitary woman farewelling her life. (I was in my teens. It embarrasses now!) And that most of the stories put together recently for a volume likewise dealt with parting. Indeed, the final lines of the final page read:

"So it's goodbye then, Lady ?"

"Yes Peter. Goodbye."

"Goodbye."

Now why had I, across almost half a century, written so persistently about Farewell, about Dispossession, about Exile and Loss and Parting of one kind or another? Mine had been an happy life enough, with no more than the usual share of leaving behind. Yet I seem to have had this deep consciousness of life as a series of ... bereavements. [AUTHOR'S EXAMPLE]

To come to understand such an unusual focus — such a vision of life's days — could well provide the stimulus for an autobiography.

Here's another:

I told Vicki yesterday about how I saw the very first motor car that came into our town. We'd known for several days that it was on its way. The telegraph kept sending reports along the route. Everyone gathered down by the Post Office, with flags, picnic baskets.

I recall it all most vividly. And that is why I am going to write down all these things that I can remember of my life while I can. Because I'm forgetting some things too. It's alarming how quickly. And arthritis is twisting and tormenting my fingers ... [AUTHOR'S EXAMPLE]

These two passages speak for themselves about "reasons". The first is the more complex. It is a specific quest, along a specific route. The second is simply an impulse to get it all down as it was, while this is still possible.

The spur for me is the fear of evaporation — erosion, amnesia. [Laurie Lee, I CAN'T STAY LONG]

Here are two others:

The purpose of this book ... is to tell the story of how a schoolboy became a professional soldier of the old Indian Army. In the course of the story I hope to have given an idea of what India was like in those last twilight days of the Indian Empire, and something more than a tourist's view of some of the people who lived there.

[John Masters, BUGLES AND TIGERS]

The main reason I put it on record was because of the early years of the Edwardian days, which were really very interesting, with a lot happening.

[Bernard Heald, TIME'S WINGED CHARIOT]

As this decision to write up your life is no light one, and will have ramifications beyond the simple sitting down and documenting past incidents, it would be sensible, before committing to record all your teeming Mondays to Sundays, to spend time clearing ground for the edifice you'll shortly construct.

This will involve some standing off from your project and surveying it. You will get an overview of what is involved in the task — why you are taking it on, how you might best set about it, where it is likely to lead you, what you might look for from it.

Such a clearing of the ground will leave you less likely to run into disorders, lost bearings, work blocks, confusions and discouragements generally. One straightforward way to set about all this is to ask of your autobiography five simple questions.

Why?...Where?.....When?......What?.....How?

The first and last — Why? and How? — are clearly the more important; but the others can yield useful insights and strategies too. So to begin....

Why?

You'll certainly not be the first to ask yourself such a question. Even the greatest:

Q. Why did I write? What sin to me unknown
Dipt me in ink ...?

A. I lisp'd in Numbers, for the Numbers came.

This question and answer, playful yet serious, is from the eighteenth century poet, Alexander Pope; and he uses "Numbers" to mean verses, rhyme.

Pope dedicated much of his writing to ridiculing fiercely the corrupt and hypocritical leaders of his day. Which made him powerful enemies, as alarmed friends pointed out. Pope was frail, tiny, hunchbacked; and retributive assault was common enough in London's dark streets.

Pope responded, in verse, to his friends' concern. Why do I write? Why plunge into ink when the consequences ...?

His answer is perhaps unexpected. He writes, he states above, because he can; and, he goes on to explain, because he must.

That is — he discovered early that he had talent; and he accepted also an obligation to employ that talent in the service of his community.

Pope was certainly able to do this. His skills with satire turned arrogant villains into objects of public derision and contempt. Much as some cartoonists manage today. He discomfited and exposed such villains to a degree that the Law, the Church and the Court simply couldn't match, those villains being:

Safe from the Bar, the Pulpit and the Throne,
Yet touch'd and sham'd by Ridicule alone.

Pope's Question and Answer are, of course, directed towards writing in general. Yet you could well see such a Question appropriate to your own project.

This so-demanding task — WHY should you be expending all these resources of energy and time (and no doubt finance!) in writing your life? Is it an interesting enough life, or an important enough one, to warrant such substantial commitment?

For most of us, the honest answer would have to be an unequivocal no! Our little lives, rounded with a sleep, are resoundingly modest. Their light imprints on the world will fade quickly over a couple of generations.

Yet despite this reality, we most of us share a conviction that there is justification for getting down on paper, with all the effort entailed, these modest lives. With autobiography we look to snatch back the spirit of those lives from the great incinerator of time!

... any bits of warm life preserved by the pen are trophies snatched from the dark, are branches of leaves fished out of the flood, are tiny arrests of mortality.

[Laurie Lee, I CAN'T STAY LONG]

So you might well feel, along with the diminutive and courageous Alexander Pope, some sort of general obligation to write your life. To make available to others, as they get on with *their* lives, the significances of your own as you see these from where you stand now.

Each life so recorded and interpreted adds something to the sum of human experience; both illuminating and enriching.

The Queensland Writers' Centre leaflet on Biography declares much the same:

Every human life is an amazing and wonderful thing worthy of being recounted and celebrated, and writing a book about one or several lives does just that.

In this sense, then, your life does take on interest and importance. The Queensland Centre statement seems also to recognise the pleasure and satisfaction to be gained from tapping your life and communicating it to the best of your abilities.

The wry converse, of course, to this proclamation of the enduring importance of humble people is the way time inexorably diminishes even the very great.

Imperious Caesar, dead, and turn'd to clay,
Might stop a hole to keep the wind away.
[William Shakespeare, HAMLET]

It might seem a little lacking in humility to link your writing aspirations with Pope's Credo that every piece of public writing should be undertaken with some sense of social responsibility. In your own life, however, you might well have had commitment to something you felt strongly about in relation to fellow human beings.

To communicate something of this commitment and of its importance to you, could be one of your reasons for writing, even if only a secondary or underlying reason. If this is so, then perhaps you should write down at this point some clear statements about what you see as your contributions to the community.

Here are a few possible areas:

- Your dedication to school teaching or nursing or any of the "service" professions. Or simply the maintaining of high standards of ethics and efficiency in, say, retailing or car repairs.
- Your crusade against proliferation of motorways, or for the preservation of National Parks.
- Your long commitment to family and provision of home.

- Your care of aged parents, or of a disabled child.
- The political oppressions you've resisted, and suffered in doing so.

By incorporating such strands into your autobiography, you are adding to those social contributions already made during your life. Your account of it now will in turn provide insight and even inspiration for others in like situations.

It could well prove useful to show to someone you respect anything you write in response to the above. This "someone" might have quite a different view of what your achievement has been in life. Which could even persuade you to revise what you've written; to extend it, qualify it; shift the weight from this to that.

It would be a good idea too to file away what you've written as well as some record of what anyone else might have commented. There will almost certainly come a point when you'll want to refer again to this material, and either feed it directly into your writing or simply allow the sentiments to permeate certain pages generally — waste nothing!

Here's an illustration of how what one puts to paper can resonate out beyond one's immediate purpose and beyond one's family and friends too. In this case, beyond even the century in which it was written!

In the early 1930s, a year or so before her death, Frances Purcell decided to write about her life. She managed some 14,000 words, in weak pencil on rough pad, about her 1870s childhood on a retail dairy in inner-city Sydney.

Although only awkwardly literate, she managed to evoke that world quite vividly: her dawn milk run under winter stars, dragging a billy-cart; her tears when one toffee-nosed customer announced her as "only the milk girl"; her mortification at having always to run to school and yet still have to sit apart at the Late Desk; her laughter at her uncle from Wales who disembarked at Circular Quay flourishing an enormous stick for, he explained, beating off the blacks; her half-amused exasperation at having to write a name-and-address label for this uncle's jacket because he could speak no English.

These amateur fragments, half a century after their authoring, proved of such interest that a university press published them, and extracts have been anthologised elsewhere. Because aged and arthritic Frances Purcell decided to write about her life, we can now get the kind of "feel", that more formal history cannot quite give us, what it was like to live a migrant childhood in Surry Hills over one hundred years ago.

Now for some of the more personal reasons for writing your life.

These vary, of course, from one individual to another. Your particular purpose will influence both what you choose to write and how you write it. That is — content and form. Here are some of the more commonly offered reasons:

- To be published and make money
- To provide some formal record for descendants
- To offer sundry information and interest for the immediate family
- As self-discovery and self-healing
- For pleasure — that is, for the kinds of satisfaction one gains from bringing some sort of order and focus to the myriad events and experiences of one's years
- Because you want to become a writer and writing your own life seems a good place to start.

To the first of these whys.

Publish and Make Money

It certainly is possible that your book will be professional enough, and you lucky enough, to attract a publisher and some sales; though it is less likely that your life will have been sufficiently glamorous or influential, or your writing skills so commanding, that you'll have all the bother of a bestseller on your hands — film rights, translation rights, all those nuisances!

To approach this in reverse: if you are a well-known politician, movie star, television celebrity, rock musician, notorious bankrupt or serial murderer, then your life could well be marketable. Then the chances are you'd be paying someone else to write that autobiography for you! Occasionally, though, someone who is relatively obscure does manage to score — as with Sally Morgan's *My Place.* I suspect that the current interest in Aborigines helped this along, its topicality.

Nevertheless, *My Place* is certainly challenging in its account of the way our original inhabitants have been (mis)treated by Europeans — even by many well-intentioned Europeans.

Albert Facey's *A Fortunate Life* has probably found even greater acclaim — certainly with me. A more simple narrative of someone's long years it would be difficult to find. This spare, plain style perfectly mirrors the plain, honest narrator. Facey is so modest and yet, in a way, heroic. His life so much a struggle; yet in his own eyes, very "fortunate".

Both the above titles are recommended as models.

There can too be publish-and-profit in what might be termed *auto-fiction* — that is, the writing up of your life experiences more in the form of fiction, using some measure of poetic licence. You still retain the first person narrator, the "I", as if all you relate really did happen to you. Which, in a way, it did.

James Herriot's *All Creatures Great and Small* is one such. No doubt Herriot rearranges and even stretches facts in these stories; but they would be a broadly reliable account of his experiences as a Yorkshire vet.

To summarise the first of these commonly offered reasons then — to be published and make money. For most of us, it wouldn't be realistic to set out to profit financially from one's autobiography. A few will do so; a few more will at least manage to cover costs. In my experience, however, few autobiographers approach their project as an entrepreneurial one. Their motives are much more likely to be personal.

A Formal Record for Descendants

This would be the least personal amongst the list. You'd basically be constructing or filling out the family tree (to employ mixed metaphors!) and getting it up to date. Naturally, you'd be heavily concerned with straight information.

This kind of pursuit sends you delving into files of papers, microfilm and other modes of information storage. You'll gather dossiers of names, dates and locations within your own life too; details of occupations and career, of residences, travel, recreations, health — all such "facts".

You'll also need to sum up the more important of your relationships — with parents, siblings, children, closer friends, perhaps some colleagues; and then to gather similar biographical facts about these people.

A sensible way to proceed would be to set up a system of folders — Me, Dad, Doris, etc. — and of titled sheets within each folder — Homes, Workplaces, Doris' Kids, etc.

Then all you already know and whatever your research turns up, you enter on the appropriate sheet and slip into the appropriate folder. The amount of information you'll eventually accumulate this way will probably surprise.

When you come to the end of this gathering-in exercise, you could set about writing it up in continuous form; a sort of formal, history-like narrative. But it would be perfectly satisfactory, if you preferred, just to tidy up what you have by typing all the bits and pieces into an ordered sequence — not forgetting to note the source for each one — and let the record stand just as it is.

If that seemed rather bare, you could perhaps write an introduction of a few thousand words, drawing attention to whatever in the records you found worthy of particular comment. Perhaps you need to give some account of how you came by certain information, particularly if this has been from relatives or friends; or a caution about those areas where the "facts" are just a little speculative. You could give suggestions as to where others might pursue further family history, such as Armagh cemetery in Northern Ireland — and, of course, some acknowledgment of any assistance received, any material belonging to others that you've used.

Most of you, however, are looking for rather more than a formal and somewhat bare record — though the above system would provide an excellent starting point for anyone, giving the orderly structure to be subsequently fleshed out.

If, though, you want to take your life and hold it up to the light, as it were; to revolve it slowly so you can see it Past, Passing and in a sense To Come; if you want to get onto paper something of the colour, shape and texture of your life, then there's more to do than just a harvesting of statistics.

This fetches us to the two remaining commonly offered reasons for writing up one's life.

Self-Discovery and Self-Healing

These two overlap in that each involves that torch mentioned earlier — journeying with it into some of the more shadowy corners of your experiences and noting and evaluating what gets illuminated there.

This will be particularly so if you are writing your life or some portion of it as in some measure *self-healing*. The life-material you employ will tend then to be restricted to whatever areas of concern are impelling you to the project in the first place.

If this area is one of major problems, even of psychic disablement, then it would seem wise to combine the guidance of writing your life with some psychotherapy. You could then discuss with your therapist what you intend to write ... and later, what you have in fact written.

Such a partnership — writing and therapist — could well prove a happy and effective one, both in terms of your psychic welfare and also in terms of the document you end up producing.

Autobiography for this purpose follows in Chapter Seven.

The broader approach, writing for *self-discovery*, can obviously hold a wide range of sub-motives — from wanting to reassure yourself that your career as senior secretary or real estate agent or mother or broker was (or perhaps was not) a worthwhile one, to simply putting down your life without any preconceived assessment and seeing what does indeed emerge.

As with for *self-healing*, there can be a practical side to this kind of autobiography.

If you know and understand something of your past, you can make more sense of your present and hence more intelligently address your future. Or to put such a thesis in reverse; unless you know where you came from, you can hardly understand much about where you are now, and certainly couldn't have much idea about where you might be heading!

There is indeed truth in the adage that those ignorant of history are doomed to relive it — personal history too!

You Wish to Become a Writer

Certainly the best authors write about what they know, about their own lives, inner and outer. Autobiographing will teach much about the skills of tapping your own experiences and of writing these up effectively.

So, to be clear about why you are setting out to write autobiography, will not only give you a light for the end of the tunnel, it will also provide some illumination for the journey through that tunnel's length and darkness.

When?

An autobiography is an obituary in serial form with the last instalment missing.

[Quentin Crisp, THE NAKED CIVIL SERVANT]

When do you sit down and write your life? At what particular point do you decide to tap into that tide? An odd question? Commonsense would seem to reply — when the life's all there, to be written. Which, of course, is patent nonsense. It would mean that the last gasp and the last full-stop would have to coincide. And even if you could organise your demise so precisely that your famous last words became the volume's final line, you'd miss all the post-writing rewards and fame!

Clearly, then, you'll be writing your life at some point before that life has concluded. Which returns us to where we started — when?

For most of us, the appropriate moment would be somewhere in the later years. By then, patterns in your life should have become visible. Your achievements, even if incomplete still, would be present in outline and in some bulk. Autobiography is most frequently, and possibly most naturally, an activity of Autumn, of Harvest Home.

It needs to be noted, though, that this isn't necessarily so. You may quite readily and effectively write autobiography at any time in your life. At some midpoint, for example. Or following some watershed event. Your work in such cases would probably comprise a summing up of one phase of your life. Most likely all those years to that point — which might well be NOW, immediately prior to your beginning to write. The work would be some sort of documenting, exploring and explaining. A clearing of the desk before moving on to the next phase of your life.

Autobiography as self-healing would frequently have this character.

Such a starting point for writing up your life-to-date, or some aspect of it, could occur when:

- You end a major relationship
- You adopt a new country
- You change careers; probably to something entirely different, and possibly involving some inner change-of-vision as well
- You are made redundant — even "sacked"
- You return to the workaday world after some overwhelming external experience, like war service, a major illness or accident, a bankruptcy, a criminal charge

- You climb back from some major retreat, like drug addiction, clinical depression, deep grief.

All these situations would provide a self-contained life-to-date. Presumably, more autobiography would follow when more life had been lived.

There is another kind of life which gets written in relatively early years, too (this one confines itself to a particular activity or feature of those years) your life as a whatever.

Test cricketers and top tennis players do this sort of thing. Their volumes cover mainly sporting experiences, paying only cursory attention to other facets of their lives, or to people who don't directly impinge on these sports activities.

Parliamentarians write of their lives as politicians; ex-employees of Buckingham Palace make fortunes; bank robbers look for a second scoop from an account of what won them fifteen years (with remissions!).

I have come across three people who have written about their lives in this way.

There was a diplomat's wife, detailing her years with displaced children in Third World refugee camps. This work hasn't found a publisher; but is well done and interesting enough and could succeed yet.

There is a retired travelling salesman (confectionery) reminiscing his quarter century driving in North East England. This work could find a publisher too; but in any case, much of it has been printed as magazine articles, and some has also been used in the after-dinner-speech circuit.

There was a ship's captain, again in retirement, who wrote a detailed and to me somewhat pedestrian account of his experiences on the high seas. This has been published and indeed has generated modest royalties.

None of the above constitute full autobiography, because each excludes so much and is so selective in what it does include. They're sufficiently writing-your-life, though, for this manual to deal with. After all, many of you might wish to concentrate on a particular facet of your life — as a teacher, doctor, clergyman, telephone technician, parent raising children on a farm, turning a derelict city block into a home-and-garden-beautiful — and to leave most other components of your life simply as frame. Think what Mrs Aeneas Gunn managed with *We of The Never Never.*

What emerges from all this is that while full autobiography is necessarily a project for the silver years, it is also both appropriate and practical to write of your life almost from the time you learn to write and have some life to provide the copy.

Indeed, in some ways the two extremes of very-late and very-early act to complement one another. To write up some aspect of your life early on is to sow obvious advantages for a more comprehensive account later.

Where?

In one sense, *where?* is much the same as *when?* (I'm ignoring the Joker who'll reply to *where?* with something like — "Not decided yet. Maybe I'll go to the top of Mount Kilimanjaro to write it.")

W*here?* could quite sensibly mean where in my own life — at what point of time in my own life — will I start writing that life?

The answer would be something like — when I turn sixty. Which is much what we've already been dealing with under *When?*

For this section, *Where?* will be understood as referring to whatever particular part of your life you elect to write about first, to open your account with.

What point of your life, what day of your life, will you lock into your first sentence?

Autobiography doesn't have to begin with Day One when you came crying hither onto this great stage of fools. Indeed, that would have to be a very poor place to begin, in a way, in that you will not be able to recreate from memory one single moment of it! You might, in fact, quite effectively begin right at the other end of your span-of-years to date. That is, from where in your life you are now. As:

> **I sit, this grey September morning, at the desk I had from my father. Beyond the great window, the garden trees stand bare; and gull cries break in upon my melancholy from cliff tops not a hundred metres beyond the front drive. Beyond again, the great Pacific stretches, uncharacteristically moveless and pewter ... and empty.**
>
> **I am wealthy now. I am very successful. I am also entirely alone. [AUTHOR'S EXAMPLE]**

Such an approach Joyce Cary employed in *To Be A Pilgrim*, where an elderly lawyer, alone in the great Devon house he spent his childhood in and in which, he knows, he is shortly to die, looks back over his life and recounts much of it. Here are the opening lines:

> **Last month I suffered a great misfortune in the loss of my housekeeper, Mrs Jimson. She was sent to prison for pawning some old trinkets which I had long forgotten. My relatives discovered the fact and called in the police before I could intervene. They knew that I fully intended, as I still intend, to marry Sara Jimson. They were good people. They saw me as a foolish old man, who had fallen into the hands of a scheming woman. But they were quite wrong. It was I who was the unfaithful servant, and Sara, the victim.**

What follows in *To Be A Pilgrim* is precisely what has been signalled in this opening paragraph — an exploration of the relationship between the narrator and Sara Jimson, across several decades.

In these two examples of starting from now and working back, I have assumed some fiction techniques. You might choose, of course, not to write in this way but in a more documentary manner, yet still to seek something of the where-you-are-now and as-you-are-now approach. So how about:

> **Today is my seventieth birthday. I find myself wealthy, very successful ... and entirely alone. [AUTHOR'S EXAMPLE]**

Of course, if you wish your life to be simply and solely record — and there are reasons aplenty why you might do so — then you'd best follow the advice given in *Alice in Wonderland:* begin at the beginning, go right on to the end, and then stop!

So far with *Where?* I've noted only two possible points of take-off — the extremes of *now* and your *birth* —and the working backwards or forwards from one of these to the other.

There could well be heaps of suitable points between these polarities from which you could launch either onwards to your present or in reverse towards your past.

Here's one, from a watershed event that has split the particular life into a before and an after:

I lived almost four decades of my life assuming, if I considered the matter at all, that cancer was what happened to other people. Mostly old people, or people who smoked, or worked in asbestos mines. But beyond all this specificity, to other people.

So when I called at the surgery for the results of the test on that small black mole, and I heard — "Melanoma. And it's reached the lymphs, I'm afraid. But there are still a number of things we can do to help you ... "

[AUTHORS' EXAMPLE]

Here's another dramatic mid-life episode used as an opening (to John Masters' *The Road Past Mandalay: A Personal Narrative*) though this does not have the "watershed" character:

Before dawn, the order reached us: the armoured cars of 13th Lancers were to make a wide outflanking movement into the desert, round the right of the enemy's position defending the small Syrian town of Deir-es-Zor. The 10th Gurkhas were to attack astride the main road. We — the 2nd battalion of the 4th Gurkhas — were to stay in camp, in reserve, at five minutes' notice for action.

There is even the possibility of that *Where?* point being before your birth or after your death; though I find it difficult to imagine an example of the latter, unless you were to dictate from Elysian Fields!

Before birth, though, is straightforward enough if it takes the form of beginning with your forebears. Here is an example from Albert Schweitzer's *My Life And Thought: An Autobiography.*

I was born on January I4th, I875, at Kayserberg in Upper Alsace, the second child of Louis Schweitzer who was shepherding just then the little flock of evangelical believers in that Catholic place. My paternal grandfather was a schoolmaster and organist at Pfaffenhofen in Lower Alsace, and three of his brothers occupied similar posts. My mother Adele, nee Schillinger, was a daughter of the Pastor of Muhlbach in the Munster Valley, Upper Alsace.

This before-birth approach was perhaps most inventively exploited in Laurence Sterne's *Tristram Shandy*, an eighteenth century pseudo-autobiography and one of the most wildly comic works in the language.

Poor Tristram tries throughout several hundred pages to get as far as an account of his birth. He never really succeeds because he keeps on sidetracking himself. He does, however, manage to record the moment of his conception, the circumstances of which, he feels, explain the chaos that both his life and his autobiography have subsequently become.

I wish either my father or my mother, or indeed both of them ... had minded what they were about when they begot me; had duly considered how much depended upon what they were then doing ...

What happened when they were "then doing" was:

"Pray, my dear," quoth my mother, "have you forgot to wind up the clock?" "Good G--!" cried my father, making an exclamation ..."Did ever woman, since the creation of the world, interrupt a man with such a silly question?"

The consequence of this conceptus interruptus?

It "scattered and dispersed" all poor Tristram's wits just as he was coming into being; so that, he explains, away these wits went, "clattering like hey-go-mad!"

Hence it was that, years later, Tristram's father would sit and lament:

"My Tristram's misfortunes began nine months before ever he came into this world."

My mother, who was sitting by, look'd up, — but she knew no more than her backside what my father meant, — but my uncle, Mr Toby Shandy, who had often been informed of the affair, — understood him very well.

I would not recommend anyone attempt autobiography in this lunatic style! It does illustrate, though, how very wide are the boundaries within which it is possible to write of your life, if you look to do more than simply marshal facts and statistics.

These said, facts and statistics are, of course, the very basis of any sound and useful autobiography; but the forms they take are many.

Even a collection of letters — letters from and letters to — can hold so many of these facts that it becomes a kind of de facto autobiography, giving a vivid and fairly comprehensive record of the letter-writer's life and times.

As a postscript — it is worth keeping in mind, if we feel like dismissing a freakish autobiography like *Tristram Shandy*, that the great Dr Johnson unwisely declared of it — "Nothing (so) odd can last".

How extensive, therefore, must be the parameters for autobiography, if one possesses the skills and imagination to exploit them.

What?

I take this question to be what — out of everything that has constituted my life — will I select to write about?

After all, you can't put down on paper your every thought and action; every situation, every moment.

Dorothy Richardson tried to do something along these lines in her twelve-volume work beginning with PILGRIMAGE. The nature of the experiment and the skill of the author make it worth reading one or two volumes; but to proceed much further is likely to leave you utterly glazed. Nor, of course, does the work anywhere-near manage to get-everything-in.

In any case, you won't be able to write up every detail of your life because you'll have forgotten most of them. As was remarked by the quirky authors of *Ten Sixty-Six And All That,* history is not what happened, it's what you can remember!

Many of you won't even want to attempt any full cover, giving equal weight to each component. You'll perforce be looking to select amongst your material. To cover those things that have been of individual importance; and those things that were fairly typical, like riding the bike to work each day: just one account of such as the latter would no doubt do as representing the lot?

Whatever — you will need some broad idea before you start of just what in your life you are looking to record and, possibly, to recreate. Then you will set out to gather up all the material you can that has to do with this.

There is a further area that *What?* can lead you into and it's the flipside of what we've been discussing.

What are you going to leave out?

I have in mind material that is personal, intimate, either to you or to others. And beyond the personal — the hurtful, even the highly destructive.

To isolate some possibilities: How frankly will you reveal your opinions of friends, relations, colleagues, neighbours? Of their actions? Their beliefs? If you do state frankly some such opinions and views, will you just leave them as stated, or proceed to justify, even document?

If the first, then you leave yourself open to charges of random and unsubstantiated malice, even libel. And in any case, if those you've mentioned unfavourably choose to respond in some way, even to defend themselves and return a few volleys in your direction — you'll have much the same decision to confront all over again: stay out of it, or start explaining?

If the second — you decide to offer reasons for criticism of, even attacks on, others — then you'll be rubbing salt into wounds already inflicted, excusable or not. It is also possible that to support your opinions you'll want to draw on information that is confidential or in some other way awkward; and this will bring in people you've chosen to leave out.

It can go on getting messier and messier!

For example — if you have had love affairs, or your partner has, will you reveal these? Or, if they have already been revealed and are in the open, will you rake them up with further detail? Will you identify the other parties, even if these were relatives, friends, close colleagues, your present employer or solicitor? Even if such persons are now in other and happy relationships, so that an entirely innocent party would be involved — perhaps children?

Even if you were only indirectly implicated in a liaison, through close friendship or family bond — would you parade that one too? Although your impulse is to eschew such revelations, your support for your friend through this quite desperate affair might have been one of the richest chapters in this friendship and merit a place, even an honoured place, in your chronicle?

Or perhaps there was a bitter family feud in which you were involved, or observed from close in, or simply took backwash from?

You could well want to outline such a feud simply to explain behaviour of your own at the time or subsequently — why you never invited Them with Them, perhaps.

Somewhat less simply: many of us have discovered that when two close friends of ours fall out seriously, it can become awkward or even impossible to continue a friendship with both. Intentionally or unintentionally, the friends just won't allow it. This is particularly so when the two estranged friends happen to have been married to each other! If you had been forced to choose between — do you attempt to explain in your autobiography why you elected to stick with one and not the other? That you'd known Richard longer? Or you thought Suzanne was the injured party?

The first of these two explanations might make not too many waves for you (though I wouldn't count on it); but the second?

There could even have been in your life some criminal or generally despicable act. This might not have been *your* act, but one of your children's, or sibling's, or partner's, or colleague's, or parents'. Or simply something you stumbled on, quite inadvertently, as:

It was about this time that, as Minister's Warden, I discovered that the Rev. Walshaw was misappropriating church funds. Not just in petty cash amounts, either.

This threw me into considerable unhappiness. I greatly admired and respected Walshaw's wife Helen; and there were also to be considered the bruises our little church community itself would sustain.

Yet there seemed no real question about what I should do.

I confronted Walshaw.

With a choice.

He chose ... to approach the bishop himself.

The scandal was a wretched one, particularly when some earlier misdemeanours came to light. Equally wretched was this cleric's continuing decline over the next several years. He was sacked yet again — by the State Government, over driving test bribes. And there was further shady dealing involving real estate. He died relatively young, and disgraced.

Helen had finally separated from him, after the driving licence episode, taking the children with her. She remarried later, and is I believe happy now in a large country house that resounds with a multitude of His and Hers. [AUTHOR'S EXAMPLE]

If this passage were from your life, would you include it? Given that, although you've been out of contact with Helen for some years, you still admired and respected her and had maintained some friendship with her throughout the exposure of the plundering of church accounts? And given also that she and her equally blameless children have moved on and away from all that dismaying past?

Such an incident would certainly have proved an important part of one's life — the suspicions, the investigation, the confirmation, the painful decisions to be made, and the distress throughout all these phases. To leave it all unrecorded would be to bury a quite significant episode ... which, in turn, would be to some extent to falsify the life.

And yet, if you include it, in all its brutality, wouldn't that also be violation of values that are embedded in your life?

Further, even if Helen wouldn't mind too much for herself — and she's the practical and honourable sort of person who well mightn't mind your publishing, as nothing of it reflects directly on her — she could well be concerned for the children. For what might get flung at them by other children, who can be so cruel.

Then, of course, the likelihood is that Helen and her circle would never hear about the book, nor see it, nor read it. So would you be justified in omitting this far-from-insignificant section from your autobiography just on the off chance that Helen *might* .... and that if she did other children *might* ... ?

I chose this example because the more consideration you give it, the more intractable it grows. The arguments seem so evenly balanced between put-it-in and leave-it-out.

It is easier to make these sorts of decisions when it is clear that to publish would definitely generate much distress or damage. Or where the material is of such overriding interest or importance that to omit, whatever reverberations threaten, would be greatly to distort or even against the common good generally. So it becomes publish and then duck! Here's another example.

My father felt he could never give the family any complete account of his genealogical researches because two unworldly sisters, living still in the age of white gloves and port wine jelly, would have been mightily upset to learn of their multitudinous convict ancestry.

In this, I believe now, he erred. To omit one's convicts would be to make a travesty of any autobiography. The sensibilities of two sweet old ladies should be — as considerately as possible — disregarded.

The film biography of Charlie Chaplin seemed to compromise itself in something of the same way. Chaplin's "interest" in young females was in his time something of a scandal. The film, however, showed the "girls" as rather older than they had in fact reputedly been. Which quite changed the significance.

To sum up then: Probably the first impulse for most of us, when faced with a decision about whether to publish something that will wound or besmirch, would be to let the dead past bury its dead. To omit what will occasion pain or uproar. After all, we've swags of other material to write up.

Such is a generous impulse; and sensible too, up to a point.

But against it — the subtraction from your account of anything of substance reduces the comprehensiveness of that account, diminishes its final value, and your integrity as author.

You might be fortunate enough to find you have no tough decisions of this kind to make. But if you're not so happily placed, then the wisest course would be to balance, calmly and responsibly, the potential for carnage against the ideals of inclusiveness and integrity.

Do the scales in your case tip at all helpfully one way or the other?

That is, would leaving out a few uncomfortable but not vitally important facts or episodes deflect considerable anger or mortification. Or would you need to omit or distort quite a deal just to circumvent some fairly minor abrasiveness?

Before finally deciding, it might perhaps help to approach any so-called victims of what you'd like to publish. To be open with them about the material and why you want to use it.

Some so approached will respond with hostility, of course; and even attempt to block any publication. I don't see that leaves you much worse off. You'll simply take the bucketing sooner rather than later.

On the other hand, many might surprise you by agreeing that the truth, however unpalatable, should stand. Or at least go in partly screened, with changes in names, dates, places, for example. Or that some of what you want to write can go in unprotested, even if the balance remains an issue to be addressed.

In any event, the courtesy of such an approach could well encourage a more considered and even more generous response, and so reduce the possibility of head-on collisions and overhasty, later-to- be-regretted, reactions.

Whatever — having followed these steps above, the weighings-up and the explainings and requestings, it would seem sensible to come to your decision about who's-in-and-who's-out and then stick with it. Only if circumstances change considerably as you write along should you fret any further.

A final caution on a fairly obvious point, from the Queensland Writers' Centre again:

> **Tempting as it may be, do not use your work to settle scores. The laws of libel are clear and the results can be very costly if they are broken.**

Even if libel laws are not directly involved, enmities aroused in score-settling can in their own ways prove equally costly to friendships and to family amities; and ultimately to your own happiness and content.

How?

The answer to this, the last of the five simple interrogatives, is what the remainder of this book deals with.

So just turn the page ...

Chapter Two

Setting Up

If you are already using an office or study and customarily do any sort of authorship in it or run some business from it, or even just have a vigorous letter-writing life, then you will need only skim this section or o'erleap it completely.

If writing is a relatively new enterprise for you, then it would be well worth your while putting thought and effort into setting up right here at the beginning. It will make the task ahead more comfortable, more productive, and more likely to prove successful.

First, of course, the obvious.

Do you have a study, or a room you could convert into one for the nonce — however long that nonce might in the event prove: an ironing/sewing room, a closed-in verandah that you can keep warm and dry, a guest bedroom? (It mightn't hurt at all to be discouraging visitors, at least until you're under weigh and into a routine with your autobiographing.) Even a more sophisticated garden shed, if it has a window and a power point for light and heating, and you can arrange some floor covering, might do.

One advantage of having a room devoted solely to your writing is that you can store all your equipment and materials there; and the latter, you can organise and file, even if only in heaps on shelves or (Heavens!) over the floor. Such heaps can really be quite handy; and because the room is yours alone, they are unlikely to be disturbed — for which read chewed by dog or vegemited by feral infant.

The second advantage of a room of your own is that after each stint there will not follow any enforced clearing up. You can leave an incomplete sheet in the typewriter, or the computer a-flicker; notes and documents all over the desk/table surface; books and papers and coffee mugs as a floor collage.

Everything is then ready for you to slip into writing mode at the next opportunity, without having to find things and sort them out and spread them into ready-set-go!

If you can't manage a room all to yourself, even if only for the duration, then a firmly designated corner of some other room is next best. I favour the main bedroom, as it tends to be large and also by its nature off-limits to callers even if less so to family.

A small desk/table in one corner with a few shelves adjacent, and you've created a mini-environment, with some seclusion and a reduced imperative to be clearing away all the time. To establish this territory by a window can be particularly pleasant; and main bedrooms frequently do have large and well-sited windows.

(Take care, though, that the outlook doesn't prove so enticing as to become a distraction. When my wife took ill once in Hawaii, the hospital gave me temporary accommodation in staff quarters; and my window and balcony overlooked the nurses' swimming pool!)

If for any reason the main bedroom proves a non-starter — as, for example, you have a spouse who takes umbrage at a typewriter clattering into his/her slumber — then a (separate) dining room, with the door closed, is another possibility.

Providing you don't entertain a great deal, or can slap an embargo on formal dinner parties for a time — so that you're not frequently packing up and clearing away — you can take over at least half the table and perhaps an end of a bookcase.

It is probably exaggeration to declare that where the will-to-write is strong, one will manage from a large crate or even within a brown paper bag! But certainly my wife and I, while earning a (precarious!) living from freelancing, would begin each working day by propelling our four youngsters off to school, then staking out a patch each end of the kitchen table and hammering away in duet from there.

The woodbox, empty patches of dresser surface and spare chairs became repositories for our paper and oddments. This strategy gave us, mostly, several hours productive peace each day.

Even more rudimentary, on a later study leave, my wife wrote up her research from a lounge chair of very pronounced antiquity and quite protean dimensions. A clearly defined area of floor became her filing shelves with a track through these for me to fetch the frequent and mandatory cups of tea.

So if you can't keep a space permanently for yourself, it's still possible to write, commandeering some bench-like space for a few hours each day. Indeed, in this age of computers, simply setting up you-and-your-computer anywhere might be enough. It can be a very individual situation, where and under what circumstances you can write.

Filing

I've already offered basic suggestions about filing. Common sense is the best guide.

Apply it right from the start — when, say, you are setting up furniture of storage and retrieval. Ponder carefully before rushing out and investing in some great cabinet with sophisticated divisions. If you can make these work for you and have the space for them — fine — your money, quite a lot of it, will have been well spent.

Many find it entirely adequate, however, and much less expensive, to use a heap of old manilla folders. Exactly what each of these is to hold tends to sort itself out as one goes along. Earlier examples will have made clear this way of doing things.

There are other methods too.

You could, for instance, designate one folder for every year of your life, as — 1941, 1942, 1943, 1944 ... NOW. That is, material as you gather it, is filed away according to the year that material relates to.

Or you could set aside one folder for every stage of your life, as — Parents, Early Family, Infancy, Youth, Adolescence, Marriage, Bankruptcy, Now, etc.

Or on a type-of-material basis, as —Printed Records, Photos, Letters, Recollections, etc.

Or by themes, as — Life Ambitions, Projects Undertaken, Losses, Relationships, Travel, Reading, etc.

For this present volume I had one folder into which I slipped everything that had to do with my introduction-to-be. As these built up, this folder multiplied into many, titled — Why? Where? When? What? How?

I kept all these folders together — with a low-tech elastic band! — with that first and general introduction folder on top, for any further thoughts that did not fit readily into any of the sub-folders. The bundle itself had a home on a bookshelf, where I could easily grab it and add something to one or other of the folders whenever such something presented; eventually, to start writing it up, folder by folder, as you see here!

Whatever method you choose for organising and exploiting your material, use something bold like a marking pen to identify each folder or shelf or file head or what-have-you. It's very trying, when using these files and records, to have to peer at undersized and indistinct identifications. Pencilled small titles can be unspeakable!

Indeed, always strive to make these minor technical components of your writing set-up as simple and friendly as possible. It saves time and effort and considerable frustration. It also proclaims a reassuring intelligence! In a word — professional.

At this point how-to-write guides usually go into considerable detail about what one might term the mechanics or technologies of getting words onto paper.

Most of this seems unnecessary. Many of you will already know something or, indeed, all about word processors and computers. Others of you will not possess either, because you have chosen not to spend the money involved, or you are not prepared to take on learning to use these machines, or you have decided that a good typewriter actually serves your needs better, as is, indeed, sometimes the case.

The above being so, a how-to specifically about computers and word processors would be the more appropriate place for such material. Here, however, are a few small general points won from experience right at the coalface.

Stationery

I divide writing paper into two categories. There is new stationery, straight out of the packaging, pristine. I reserve this pretty much for final copy, what one eventually submits to publishers or circulates around the family traps, or for correspondence.

There is also the paper on which I work. And as I can only type/scribble on one side at a time, it doesn't the least matter what's on the other side. Hence I use the backs of:

- Fair copy I've spoiled and abandoned, or made changes on and retyped on another page.
- Photocopy sheets not up to the mark, and so discarded.
- Unsolicited A4-sheet mail from real estate agents solicitous of selling/buying me a house; broker reports of glittering sharemarket opportunities; all such, provided they're blank one side.

Such strategy provides me with "working paper", which cuts down expenses; and takes some pressure off our beleaguered forests too.

Words to Paper

Use whatever means to "write" that suits you. The last thing you want is to be distracted by pen/typewriter/word-processor/cassette recorder that impedes or irritates you.

Don't feel Neanderthal if you prefer simple handwriting-onto-pad. Likewise, you should not feel a trendy exhibitionist if you go in for a sophisticated computer.

Be not the first to welcome in the new,
Nor yet the last to bid the old adieu ...
[AUTHOR'S EXAMPLE[1]]

... doesn't apply here! To rewrite the above as statement rather than as exhortation: some writers prefer simple long-hand still, while others do it "no hands" — they dictate. It's a free country. (well, fairly, at the moment).

More and more, though, writers are enthusing about word-processors (including the word-processing component of computers), particularly for the rewriting and editing and storage features these have.

Sometimes, however, operations are simpler/quicker on an electronic typewriter — a small correction on a single page, for example, or moving around a lot between single and double spacing. And there are traps, too, with word-processors; the unwary calamitously annihilate large parcels of deathless prose.

I suppose the sensible position would be this, that if you propose more than this autobiography, and if you already have a modicum of office skills, and if you can afford the outlay, and if the prospect of some hours of learning-how-to-use does not overly dismay you — then you could do a lot worse than invest in the technology. And, of course, if you can already touch-type, you'd be half way there.

As an example of compromise in all this: I first roughed these lines in longhand; very rough, from an old chair on the verandah. I then put them through the electronic typewriter, expanding and editing and polishing. This final version is going through the word processor, as it is, on balance, easier to make editorial changes and to retain "fair copy" there.

I often find pen better in the early stages, particularly if material is coming grudgingly, and/or I've heaps of cross-outs and swooping arrows.

---

[1] A variation on a quote from Pope's *"Essay on Criticism"* 1:335

I can cross and swoop on typescript too, but increasingly these days I'm moving straight from pen to wordprocessor.

My wife mostly works straight onto her fairly simple word processor.

I have found, over several decades, that it's wise to keep all rejected or reworked pages for quite some time, in a large cardboard carton, perhaps. It's surprising how often one wants to go back to these. (Once your autobiography is finished, you can turn the contents of this carton into the backs-of-sheets uses.)

If you are working on disc don't forget to keep two back-ups. Perhaps your most recent version vanishes. Or you might decide you actually did it better the first time round. Or there's a reference you noted but forgot to transfer.

Make sure that all round you on the desk and shelves, you set out every bit-and-piece you are likely to need — pens, pencils, rubbers, correction fluid, adhesive tape, slide-on paper fasteners, scissors, stapling machine, scribble paper, (salted nuts ...).

One simply cannot concentrate effectively if continually distracted by having to stop and search around for minor essentials.

How-to-write guides will also tell you to put aside set times for your writing slot each day. This is excellent if you can manage it, because we do get conditioned thus. The creative juices, you might say, are likely to switch on at such timed points, and to flow.

Some of us, however, simply can't guarantee such a regular slot. Much of our day gets already spoken for by our jobs, our domestic round, our wider family responsibilities.

We have then to reconcile ourselves to writing as opportunity offers, striving for whatever regularity our circumstances do allow. Alternatively, we can transfer the daily stint into the (for others) sleeping hours of, for example, 5.00 a.m. to 6.30 a.m.

My wife and I used to do this in our younger days. It did catch up with us, though, and we were not able to build such a procedure indefinitely into our diurnal round. Others do succeed.

When getting "your time" proves unacceptably difficult, it is even more important to strive for a study dedicated solely to your writing. And to get family and friends to understand and accept this.

In such a designated study, or best substitute, you gain seclusion. You also have everything in the room, all the associations there, urging you gently to drift off into that world where line flows on line. That's the theory anyway!

I met an American writer once who, when writing at home proved impossibly difficult, booked himself and his load into a hotel for a stint of a fortnight. He would write ten hours a day then visit home. I think I'd rather get up at 5.00 a.m.!

If you are determined enough, then whatever the logistical problems you encounter, you will get by and fill lots of pages.

One final point to do with the mind-set for setting up. It's of primary importance, beginning an autobiography, to be looking to the long haul. Occasionally such a work — though I'd suspect of questionable quality — has been produced over a few furious weeks.

It is more realistic to be looking at a year, say, or even to a venture that will set you back still longer.

This is due to the nature of the task, the gathering up, the planning, the sorting out, the putting together, the writing up, the editing, perhaps the marketing.

Patience and persistence will, I am convinced, stand you in better stead than will spasmodic Herculean bursts or indeed than prodigious literary talent alone.

If it's an enjoyable and absorbing enterprise, then you would want to savour it rather than rush through it, anyway.

Chapter Three

Starting Writing

I suppose that if any how-to-write text comes to a crunch at some point, here would be the place for this one — even if you've been keeping a journal for years and so have to-hand heaps of the most appropriate material of all.

And the crunch — is how do you get those first few lines of autobiography onto all that empty white paper?

If you should already have an opening sentence spilling from you, if subsequent sentences seem eager to burst out across page one, then fine. Get them down before they lose themselves amongst all the clamour of your day's demands.

Indeed, if it still all runs free for you, keep right on writing! While Dame Fortune favours you thus, the momentum might swing you right to the end of your task, leaving only the tidying up and, of course, the rewards.

For most of us though, those first lines won't offer themselves as sweetly as that. We'll have to get started some other way.

One proven approach is simply to begin by writing down, more or less at random, any material to do with your life that comes to mind. Write down any small bricks of information you can recall about your years; scenes, people, places you've visited, houses you've lived in, objects you've owned, cars you've driven, people you've liked — or haven't liked — even things you've dreamed about.

Enough of such bricks and you've built that wall termed your autobiography.

Here's a general example that explains itself:

David and I were very young when Nessie was born, but we were happy with each other and Nessie was a much loved and wanted baby. There was no suggestion of my working, except for helping out at David's school, teaching things like sewing to the girls (customary for the teacher's wife at such "small schools"), so there were no pressures to take me away from looking after Nessie and I enjoyed being a young Mum. We had very little money — David's Aunt Val lent us a bit to buy "Apple Cottage" — but I had tons of baby clothes, absolutely lovely clothes as Nessie was the first grandchild on either side. Nellie and Ellie made beautiful clothes. Besides, in those days of extended family, the arrival of a baby was a very important event, and I was given loads of presents from Nellie's sisters and cousins, to say nothing of their friends and even "the tennis ladies". And Aunt Val's friends too, and of course my own friends. David and I led a quiet but contented life at "Apple Cottage". It was a little, century-old, slab-log building of four rooms, with roofed open verandahs front and rear. David and his father had to do quite a bit of work to get it habitable for our arrival — baby's and mine; because it didn't have a bathroom, nor indeed any kitchen floor! They got it shipshape — old palings for that floor, and a pit toilet at the end of the back garden; and installed a fuel stove in time for us and Nellie to arrive, when Nessie was a fortnight old. There was no electricity, but we had a Tilley and other lamps, and we later obtained a kerosene fridge. Nellie stayed with us for two weeks, just to help out: she just adored Nessie. So of course did Ellie and Bill; but they weren't as free to help us in this way. I think David's father probably came up at weekends. He was a lovely, kindly, self-effacing man with a beautifully dry sense of humour. He seemed to like me well and we all got along nicely. The Blue Mountains were absolutely gorgeous in March when we arrived, and my recollections of that period are of a very happy time. [AUTHOR'S WIFE'S EXAMPLE]

Such an approach acts to shore up your confidence for a start, because there, right in front of you, pages of sorts start piling up and you are reassured that you at least have something.

You should also start to feel that what you're doing isn't all that difficult. Even more encouraging, you should begin to realise that what you're getting behind you is probably the more difficult part of the project. What still lies ahead — selection amongst this material you've written; editing, putting it all into order — will almost certainly prove easier than this filling up of blank pages; the manufacture of something out of complete nothing.

Writing down such recollections and episodes could even suggest an overall structure to you — the way you'll organise them eventually in your volume.

That is, which might go where. Which recollections/episodes seem to cluster together and so offer a natural chapter, perhaps.

Fasten any such together immediately, before they do a Diaspora on you. You will then also have gone some distance towards addressing the question of what sort of architecture your autobiography should have.

So begin by simply writing things down, just as these present themselves.

It won't matter how long you keep on doing this — weeks, even months — it's all bricks; and the mortar, later on, presents much less of a task.

Refuse to be intimidated by what might increasingly come to resemble an intractable ragbag of shredder material. It isn't. It's unprocessed gold!

Indeed, even write it all in letter form, if that would seem to make it easier. Tell it that way, to someone real or imagined who would he interested. Even write to yourself!

(The first such piece quoted in this chapter was written in something of that way: as if Nessie had asked her mother for an account of her infancy and childhood.)

Anyway, here are some sources you might tap for this writing-things-down stage.

Earliest Memories

All the sun long it was running, it was lovely, the hay

Fields high as the house, the tunes from the chimneys, it was air And playing, lovely and watery

And the fire green as grass.

And nightly under the simple stars

As I rode to sleep the owls were bearing the farm away,
All the moon long I heard, blessed amongst stables, the nightjars

Flying with the ricks, and the horses

Flashing into the dark.

[Dylan Thomas, FERN HILL]

You might finally not want to use all you jot down here; but get as much as you can down anyway, it can be important. Often it will all expand as you write, as more flows back to you both of incident and of atmosphere accompanying it.

I first recall playing in my front street, an unpaved cul-de-sac of sand and flat stone. I'd make houses there out of matchsticks, and mini-roads between these. Create a busy little universe all of my own.

Looking back to that infant semi-fantasy, I can see that I still do something of the same.

I organise my own immediate environment — over-organise it, my daughters charge! And move around fairly self-containedly within it; the imagination still a major factor there. And I still enjoy dealing with what is tactile and of nature — gardens, wood heaps, hammer and plank, ladder and paintbrush. Even cooking! [AUTHOR'S EXAMPLE]

Do any of your earliest memories seem to have significance like that? Existing not simply as themselves, as particular record; but additionally, as foreshadowing directions and some essential features of your character and life?

These would be the ones to flush out. They then lead your writing on to later, and to connecting, years and episodes. And they might highlight those later years-and-episodes to an extent that coming to them unannounced would not match. That sense of one thing growing out of another; of initial promises realised; of the-child-is-father-to-the-man kind of set-up.

It works to add coherence to any full account of your life.

Another of my most vivid earliest memories is of returning protesting to Kindergarten after some weeks of absence with whooping cough, and dragging an elderly teacher down the building's main entrance steps. I choose not to speculate on any prefiguring character this episode might have held!

Virginia Woolf, in *A Sketch Of The Past*, tells of her first memory in this way:

> **This was of red and purple flowers on a black ground — my mother's dress; and she was sitting either in a train or in an omnibus, and I was on her lap. I therefore saw the flowers she was wearing very close; and can still see purple and red and blue, I think, against the black; they must have been anemones, I suppose.**
>
> **Perhaps we were going to St Ives; more probably, for from the light it must have been evening, we were coming back to London. But it is more convenient artistically to suppose that we were going to St Ives, for that will lead to another memory, and in fact it is the most important of all my memories ... It is of lying half-asleep, half-awake, in bed in the nursery at St Ives.**
>
> **It is of hearing the waves breaking, one, two, one, two, behind the yellow blind. It is of hearing the blind draw its little acorn across the floor as the wind blew the blind out. It is of lying and hearing this splash and seeing this light, and feeling, it is almost impossible that I should be here; of feeling the purest ecstacy I can conceive.**

Mrs Woolf's fiction demonstrates that the sea and these early waves were indeed a seminal memory for her. They later came to represent life. The way each individual wave gathers up out of formless and impersonal ocean; grows upward and moves forward; and finally collapses onto wide sands, to return forever to that formlessness and anonymity from which it rose.

Her most ambitious novel, in fact, is titled *The Waves*; and ocean and its waves sound throughout what is often regarded as her most successful novel, *To The Lighthouse*.

Don't overlook your earliest memories of people, particularly of your parents.

It could be interesting at this point to line up these first memories of particular people with your later, more adult memories of them.

Were your parents much the same for you at the start as they, in fact, turned out to be in later years? Or did you over time come to realise you needed to modify these early impressions and judgements?

You might get a few paragraphs like these:

I recall my father as tall, upright, quiet, watchful. Something of a figure of Justice. Whereas my mother was petite, with crimped blonde curls, blue eyes, laughter, ready tears, and arms open and often floury. More like Mercy?

It was not till I was much older, in late teens, that I became aware of the deceptiveness of these first appearances. That, indeed, and somewhat ironically, these roles applied rather more in the reverse.

My tall father's silences were nearer to self-effacement, even retreat. His watchfulness and kindly concern actually held a wariness, one based on many a blustery experience.

It was more my mother who was Justice; even The Avenger! The quick, fierce shake of those curls. The blue eyes ... instant ice! The laughter that could quickly, unpredictably, flash to scorn. Those arms, reassuringly floury and all, could snap into reverse and sweep away rather than embrace. And the tears? They were likely to transfer in the instant to my own infant orbs. [AUTHOR'S EXAMPLE]

This is, like the Woolf, a somewhat literary example; and you might not choose to write with such flourish. It does indicate in principle, though, how many are the ways you can take off from some of these earliest memories.

Some of such memories of things and of people can be drawn together into a visual rendering of first scenes.

First Scenes

Quite a deal of copy could emerge from this. Indeed, it's possible you'll never get to use all of it; but this is no disadvantage. To have a pool of scenes ready to draw on allows you to choose those of most colour and of overall significance, which in turn will increase the general readability and value of your autobiography. It will also give you practice in the writing of succinct and effective paragraphs.

Here's one:

My cousin George joined me out on the back lawn. He picked up a stone; tossed it straight into the air.

It came down precisely on his own head.

George's instant bellow flushed out both his father and his mother. He told them I had thrown the stone at him.

I explained exactly what had happened.

"I prefer to believe George," my uncle declared loftily.

Old Mrs Haines, who had been in her yard next door hanging washing, had witnessed both the incident and my protests. She confirmed my account. But —

"George does not lie," my uncle reiterated. And he and Young Master Truthful gathered up their indignation and departed.

Thus did Life-Capital-L proclaim to me its complete indifference to both Truth and Innocence.

[AUTHOR'S EXAMPLE]

George, incidentally, went on lying intermittently through all the standard Seven Ages of Man, including two collapsed marriages and several ditto de factos. All the relationships had seemed to me to be with basically decent women who simply expected from him some measure of acceptance of responsibility and integrity. UNtruth will out?

Anyway, in such a manner you could tap your own earliest memories directly. You'll quite likely generate some knock-on effect, as one recollection bumps off another, like a line of railway carriages when the first takes a shunting hit.

There are also less direct ways of uncovering this elusive most-distant-past. Here are some.

Old Photos

These can restore quite an astonishing amount of what has seemingly gone forever. Two examples.

When sifting through some of the detritus from my mother's estate I came across a small, faded and much creased sepia snap of me as a toddler on the back step, with Teddy.

I confess, sadly, that Teddy generated not a flicker. He had departed forever into that Great Oblivion where even the most revered of Teddies wind up, along with all associated cute anecdotes.

But that back step on which I sat did do some activating; and I recalled that not long after this rendezvous with young Teddy, a sunroom was constructed over the site.

Why I recall this isn't entirely to my credit. It is because my mother made a batch of wondrous lamingtons for the builder — my Uncle Ben actually — and I was extremely miffed about it because she never ever made lamingtons like that for me!

My second example is more of recollecting a state, of a Spirit of the Age, than of one particular incident.

Old photos keep turning up here of family groups posing self-consciously on a lawn, with apparently ubiquitous flowering hydrangeas in the background.

Prominent too are the Aunts, amply bosomed, hats ostentatiously feathered.

These recently happed-on photos act to confirm what I'd come increasingly to believe over several decades — that my early years were dominated by big women with quite intimidatory confidence in their substance and rectitude.

Indeed, my wife has come to term the whole thing "The Family Hydrangea Factor!"

I should in fairness add that I do also owe to these formidable would-be-matriarchs my strong attraction to language and literature and a sense of responsibility to community. But they imposed, and perhaps bequeathed, many subtle arrogances and tyrannies too!

Old Formal Records

These can sometimes be surprisingly fruitful.

Again, two examples; this time from an Aunt's estate.

The first was from a file of acrimonious correspondence between Aunt Meg and the local Council over the construction of a driveway. The Council, as was usual with my Aunt, capitulated.

This in turn brought back to me one whole minor but vivid stream in my life — this Aunt feuding with almost every authority and neighbour that fell in her way (or driveway!). As she was my godmother, and lived but two minutes walk from my home, this contentiousness not infrequently managed to involve me too, in some inescapable way. It became, right up to her death when she was tangling with her surgeon over the account and I was pressed to intervene, one of the more fractious corners of my own life.

In fact I have just this moment remembered — an example of how one recollection calls up another — that Aunt Meg was the only ratepayer in the area, so far as I could discover, who won from Council the privilege of having garbage men climb more than thirty steps twice a week to collect her bin — on the grounds that she was too infirm to carry it down the steps herself.

I'm remembering too, now, how very "careful" she was with expense. I choose that term advisedly — she was not in the least mean, indeed on occasions quite otherwise; but almost grotesquely careful.

She sent me out once to pick "nine beans" for herself and a friend. (Who got four and who five, I never discovered.) When she was in an hospice, dying, she continued her daily Scotch and soda, having a niece fetch in the soda in clusters-of-four. The day before she died, she whispered to my cousin — "Just bring in the *one* bottle of soda tomorrow, Love."

Well, why waste three on nurses?

The second example: amongst Aunt Meg's effects was a small square of coarse cardboard, cut from some packet, and used as a postcard. The postmark was simply "Turkey, June 24, 1915".

Dear Meg, Thank you for the letters. We are in the trenches and have now been here a month. I can tell you we are glad to get a little news from Epping now and again. We are all in good health. Excuse P.C., because it is the only kind we get here. I wish to be remembered to all your people.

Yours truly,

I asked my mother, still alive then, about this.

She recalled the young man, but not his ever having displayed any particular interest in Meg, who had a reputation even then of being somewhat more than ornery. But she did remember him dancing once with their mother shortly before embarking for the War; and at the end of the dance he'd exclaimed — "Mrs Purcell, you dance divinely."

Whether this was in a spirit of teasing, or genuine admiration, the incident provided me one more small brushstroke to the picture of Family Past.

None of this added to my memories of World War I — I can have none, I was not born till long after the last guns fell silent, though in good time to hear those of World War II open up — but it did a little intensify the impact of our photo of my wife's Uncle Sonny, facing the camera stiffly in his puttees and Sam Brown.

Sonny fell at Passchendale. There is no one alive any more to whom he can be other than an awkward young man in an awkward pose in a faded photograph, named Walter, in its diminutive, Sonny.

I add to the above a small cedar box from Uncle Bert, full of his War memorabilia; discharge papers, Gallipoli medal (he fought there with the English contingent, emigrated to Australia later) and such sad detritus.

Then there were tales from my father-in-law, who was with the occupying troops in France following the Armistice. The last years of his life he talked — indeed, confided — a lot about his experiences there. There'd been quite a few episodes that, sensibly, he'd never passed on to Nana!

Now these and several like-items could all come together in an autobiography in a section, a small one, dealing with the effects of the Great War on the lives of me and my parents, reared as we were in either its approaching or retreating shadow. Because it certainly was a watershed event — a watershed catastrophe! — in our Western Civilisation's history.

My parents and their crowd swung into that conflict with supreme confidence in their world and its values, and in the rightness of the Allied cause. Poor little Belgium — this is your Flag — your King calls YOU! Etc.

Then the casualty lists began appearing, pages of them daily; and reports filtering back from the trenches, with the mud and cold, corpses and rats. The massive battles where young men in their tens and even hundreds of thousands were cut down by machine guns or fragmented in the artillery barrages. Mostly without either side gaining much advantage.

The initial great optimism and faith became overwhelmed by enormous horror, and an almost drowning sense of pity and even futility, amongst those of intelligence and sensibility anyway.

That's the world — blasted apart, bleeding, disillusioned and, post-War, almost frenzied in its pursuit of pleasure — in which my parents and their families and friends married, produced children and set about getting on with their lives.

Plus there was the Great Depression, of course. The world I inherited and was born into.

I couldn't attempt to understand the shape and trajectory of my own life without first comprehending something of those twin platforms from which, and into which, I was initially launched.

Whether you yourself will want to explore this Zeitgeist, this Spirit of the Times, surrounding your birth, is something you'll have to decide for yourself.

Old Folks

The older you are, of course, the fewer old folks there'll be around for you to consult. Indeed, some of you might well be already blessed with old folk status yourself!

Still, however many years you wear, there'll always be someone around whose recollections stretch even further into that dark backward and abysm. Indeed, even contemporaries might be able to fetch up memories that have fled you; or at least of events in which you didn't directly participate.

A lot of information can just drop unsought from oldies, like ripe fruit from trees, when you are having the most casual chat — particularly if you are alert enough to give that tree something of a shake when opportunity seems to offer.

Here's an example.

I'd been led to believe all my adult life that Billy Hughes, Prime Minister of Australia at the end of World War I, had some connection with my family. One suggestion was that they'd all emigrated from Wales in the same vessel. I checked that: it wasn't so. Eventually, I decided the alleged link was fabrication; though why such a fabrication baffled me.

Then, towards the end of her life, when my mother's mind was randomly tossing fragments around in her long memory, she remarked apropos of nothing:

> **Billy Hughes came round one day and said to my grandmother: "Mrs Lepherd, lend me seven and sixpence to buy a horse." And my grandmother said: "Here's ten shillings, Billy. Buy a decent one."**

I went and checked addresses of both parties late nineteenth century, and sure enough my great grandmother and the young William Morris Hughes had lived within a block of each other in East Sydney. I've little doubt that the anecdote is true.

One cannot, of course, simply wait around for items like this to waft one's way. It is necessary also to set up more structured interview situations — taking care not to have these getting intimidatingly formal — over a coffee or a drink, perhaps, or a leisurely wander around some familiar garden or park or beach, or a taking-out-to-lunch.

The secret of getting information from such interviews lies in preparation. Get very clear on what areas you are researching. Have some specific questions about each of these. Refresh your mind with whatever background you have already.

Of your mother, for instance: "Do you remember Mother when I was an infant? Was her hair coppery then — I've only seen black and white photos — curled? What style? Did she read historical romances then? How did she and Dad meet? Court? What did their parents think of them then? What sort of things would she have done while Dad was at work? Did she play tennis then? Have favourites amongst us children? What made her laugh? Angry? What did she and Dad talk about? Did they have any politics? Who were their friends? When they went out together, where would it have been to? How would they travel? Her favourite kinds of clothes? Did she have tea without milk and sugar then? How did she and Aunt Meg get on in those days? Did she ever say anything in particular about me? Ambitions for me? Fears about me? What did she feed us? I recall my father being sent out to buy 'six pennyworth of bruised fruit'. Can you explain?"

You went down to the tram lines and rubbed black grease all over your teeth. When you smiled, your mother almost had hysterics: thought your teeth had been knocked out!

Your mother used sometimes to refer to your pushy and overdressed Aunt Delia as "The great Mrs Robinson in her skunk fur coat." When you answered the door once — to Aunt Delia — and your mother asked who it was, you shouted back, "It's the great Mrs Robinson in her skunk fur coat." [AUTHOR'S EXAMPLE]

Such persistent questioning can unearth characters and days that would otherwise remain lost forever.

You could question about your infant self too, if the aged person you are interviewing is rich enough in years to have been around and aware at the time of your debut.

"Was I born bald? What was my father's response to my birth? How did I get my name? Did I have any particularly idiosyncratic ways of behaviour? Or of responding to others' behaviour? Any fetching mannerisms? Any Demon qualities? Likes and dislikes amongst foods, games, locales, weather, ways of getting to sleep, toys, people? What about Infants' School? Sunday School? It's said I specially loved my grandmother ... ?"

Such patient and imaginative probings, well prepared initially, provide pages of material about times quite beyond your own recall; yet your times, nonetheless.

It would obviously be profitable to exploit old folk and old photos simultaneously, letting them generate your past one out of the other.

"In this group — who's that young woman? That dog? Who else lived at Cronulla then? What happened to them? That shawl in the Christening photo — where did it come from and where is it now? That photo of a timber covering over a well — I've this faint recollection of putting my foot through rotten boards somewhere like that. Know anything about it? That print of 'Jethro's Daughter' on the wall in Aunt Meg's loungeroom — why wasn't it there when she died? Those steps at the side of the lawn — they're in the middle now. Why and when were they switched?"

Old Things

It can pay off handsomely to ask about these too.

For instance, there had always been in my home a whole shelf of blue volumes, the complete works of Edward Lord Lytton, a Victorian novelist highly regarded once though the long, prosy tales are little read any more.

I'd a vague idea they were something special in my father's eyes; but it wasn't until long after his death that I asked about them and learned that they were a gift from my mother, in particularly romantic circumstances.

The ever-present china cabinet can unearth a swagful of memories too — in your parents' home and in those of relatives — wedding presents and birthday gifts, heirlooms and trophies and collections.

Insist on a provenance for each item.

"How did that handle get broken? What's the significance of that odd design on Mum's jewel box? Why Welsh hats? How does Meg come to have five silver teasets from India? Aunt Sylvia's doll collection? Why would Uncle Ted have pipes there? I never ever saw him smoking?" Each of the questions above — ones I actually have asked — should draw out information often minor but almost always of sufficient interest to be worth recording for possible inclusion in your "story".

Those five silver tea sets above, for example:

Aunt Meg, as recounted earlier, could be both quite generous and almost grotesquely "careful". So, although she travelled around the world a good deal, it was almost a *sine qua non* with her that she would visit only places where people would accommodate her virtually free.

In India, there was a mission in the mountains back of Darjeeling where she could stay in return for some small services back in Australia; hence she visited there a number of times.

Meg's characteristic scrutiny of set-ups and their possibilities soon discovered that Indian and Australian Government regulations permitted her to fetch back old silver tea services largely free of taxes and duties. This, given the initial low purchase price, made them splendid gifts — expensive here but very cheap indeed for Meg to obtain.

This, anyway, is what the family have surmised. Though why none of the tea services seem indeed ever to have translated into special gifts, I don't know? Perhaps Meg came to think no occasion worthy of so costly (Australian price) a gift? At her death they went to the two legatees at a rate of two and a half Indian silver tea services each!

After china cabinets, try wall decorations, pictures, drapes, tapestries, artefacts.

"That's from when your uncle and I went to Italy in 1937. You wrote that your teacher said Mussolini was a bad man so we should come home."

Quite a deal about my primary school anti-fascism — naive and ill-informed, but basically spot on — emerged from this interview. My aunt had been quite tickled about it, apparently, especially in the light of later world events.

Are there any picture rail platforms holding similar oddments, old newspapers or trade journals or Parish Messengers or school magazines or simply clippings?

The reasons for the preservation of these will likely be self-evident — a report of some family event or family achievement, a wedding or funeral or christening or birthday party? Perhaps there was a great deluge, or fire, or filling in of a quarry where, contrary to all instruction, you used to play; a letter to an editor or speech to some group; an article you or some family member had published; most likely of all, I suppose — an obituary.

If the reasons for the printed material isn't obvious, ask around. I did not understand why a cousin's drawer held, deep down, an account-with-photo of a great liner stranded in the middle of the Great Australian Bight. Questioning revealed that my cousin and her husband-to-be had not only been on that hapless vessel but also that Jim had improved those shining few days by courting and (successfully) proposing to my cousin.

Jewellery also provides a source of earliest memories and of information generally. Proceed with this much as with the other material above.

Old Boxes and Packets

These lie around under the bed in the spare room, up in the loft or attic, at the backs of less frequently opened drawers, in a corner of the study under that sewing machine no one uses any more or under the stairs, in the garden shed or garage or tool shed, even under the house or up in the roof.

You may come across masonic regalia; flower show awards; CWA awards; parish council minutes; recipe collections; Gran's poetry; address books; old flowers; even a wedding posie; funeral "tributes" or one sort and another; Uncle Arthur's aborted attempt at autobiography; notes for a speech; business cards; postcards; telegrams of congratulation, condolence, anger, forewarning; passports and itineraries; receipts; elephantine cheap jewellery; shopping lists; memos; tickets — for travel, entrance, the raffle/lottery; and that final great category of — too-numerous-to-mention!

The plundering of such boxes and packets and drawers (for information only, of course) might need to be done tactfully. The Past Private and even more the Past Painful is often entrusted to such repositories. The potential for information about your life and times is considerable.

Old Letters and Diaries

This can be a tricky area.

For a start, there mightn't *be* any old letters or diaries. It can hardly come much trickier than that!

Even when, as mostly, there is such material about, should you plunge in and read it all, private lines by others? (Your own, of course, present no problem so far as reading them goes — apart perhaps from acute embarrassment!)

If you do decide a particular swag of such writing might invade the privacies of folk still living, how can you know, without at least glancing through it first? To say nothing of further considerations about using the material in your autobiography.

No how-to manual can resolve this problem. It's one for manners and values, not writing methodology. But here are a few guidelines.

If there are others living who have an interest in, say, letters, it would be courtesy to consult with them early on. I use "interest" here in the quasi-legal sense of some actual claim upon the letters from their family relationship or because of something in the contents, not just in the sense of "interesting for them to read".

If it seemed reasonable, you could undertake not to quote directly from these letters, nor to use information gained from them without permission from others involved. That way, you can begin by using the letters exactly as you see fit; then, later, check with those others involved to see whether you need to trim back at all. After all, why invite hassle over items you finally mightn't want to include anyway?

Such a procedure tends to allay suspicions and alarm. Quite often, when those concerned see what you've actually written and how it fits in with your other material, they find your use of the letters justifiable and perhaps not so very threatening after all.

Sometimes, though, no one else is directly involved. The writers' addressees, and those getting honorable or infamous mention in the letters, are dead or gone-to-Alaska. No one remains warm above ground to object to anything published.

There can still remain constraints of good taste.

I had to confront this when, in my mother's estate, I came across two dozen love letters to her from my father. They were written in about the third year of their marriage, when the first child had been stillborn and my mother was in a convalescent home briefly.

The letters are tender, wonderfully silly at times, occasionally intimate. I was not at that point writing anyone's life, so there was no question about publication. It was simply a matter of deciding what to do with them. As I saw it, I could:

- **Destroy them**. This would safeguard my parents' privacy fully and irreversibly and forever. But all that affectionate foolery, to ashes? It seemed barbarian! The letters were so revelatory of that rich human soil in which I took my being and prospered.

- **Retain them then, but forever unread?** Then pass them on to my estate, to remain likewise forever undestroyed but unread still? This seemed, not to put too fine a point upon it, damned stupid.
- **Read them**, enjoy them for what they wonderfully were, honour them? And invite my children, in due course, to do the same and at an appropriate time, my grandchildren. Even, perhaps, several close friends who knew and loved my parents?

From the tone in which I've set out these choices, you'll probably realise which one I took. I remain happy with it. It's a decision which celebrates affection. I hope that my parents, from wherever they blow now in viewless winds around the pendant globe, would agree.

Here's a postscript to the above. In my study I've a small trunk holding several hundred letters my wife and I exchanged in the two years before we married, when I was teaching at a remote bush school. We wrote almost daily!

We've made clear to our children that at our cease these letters are for whomever amongst them can be bothered with them. They've been warned though that few real blossoms of the heart are to be discovered from under that rusty lid.

One final point about the several forms of old written records: There are, obviously, two ways in which you can employ these. You can quote them directly. Or you can simply give a paraphrase or summary of their contents.

Hence if you are at all uneasy about quoting directly, it could well prove wiser to compromise with just a more general reference to your material. If even this becomes sticky and a worry, I'd be inclined to forgo the particular item altogether unless it is of surpassing importance. To proceed only with anxiety would be to forfeit much of the satisfaction you might properly expect from writing your autobiography.

For most of this section, you'll have noted, I've concentrated on getting started from relatively early information. Experience has demonstrated that this comes easiest for many people, perhaps because it is more remote and less personal; or because it seems more romantic! It's an area that has to be researched at some stage anyway; and to do so first-up often provides shape and direction for writing about later times in your life.

The important thing is — ***start writing.***

Chapter Four

Getting it Together

I had first intended this chapter to be titled "Putting Chapters Together"; but that seemed at the same time both too wide and too narrow.

It's *all* your material that has somehow to be got satisfactorily together, not just material for each chapter.

Sometimes you'll be wanting to gather items up into small, cohesive sections within chapters.

At the other extreme, you'll be looking for the chapter blocs themselves to come together in a unified whole; to have the completed book itself, a work that embraces all your material, all the minisections and chapters.

> **If a book is to stand, one must first choose its shape — the house that the tale will inhabit. One lays out the rooms for the necessary chapters, then starts wondering about the furniture. The moment before writing is perhaps the most harrowing of all, pacing the empty rooms, knowing that what goes in there can belong nowhere else, yet not at all sure where to find it. There are roofless books in all of us, books without walls and books full of lumber. I realized quite soon, when writing my own, that I had furniture to fill a town. [Laurie Lee, I CAN'T STAY LONG]**

What this amounts to, then, is organising your material. Indeed, "Organising Your Material" could also have been a satisfactory title for this section. Obviously you're not going to write up your material in the order in which it came to you from your researches, or the order in which you picked it up from your desk.

So — *how?*

There are, as implied earlier, two distinct approaches here. You can set your material out in the sequence in which the events of your life in fact occurred.

This is the *chronicle approach.* The most straightforward example I know is that of the Anglo-Saxons, all those centuries ago. Their earlier Chronicles simply state the year and then begin — "Her ... " That is, "At this place (in the annals ...") — and then list the battles, raids of plunder, deaths of kings and churchmen, falling stars — virtually without any comment. Only by inference from what has been considered worth the recording can one have any idea of what the writers might have thought about what was happening in their time.

An alternative approach is to set out your material around ideas, central events or some sort of viewpoint.

This might, rather loosely, be termed a *thematic approach.*

Probably the first approach, the chronicle, is easier, as the material pretty much strings itself out along that time line, and you simply write it in the order in which it happened.

The second approach, the thematic, might prove the more interesting for the reader and convey the significances of a life more adequately. It does, though, require a lot more organisation of the material.

In either case, of course, a great deal depends on the quality of the writing, and I suppose on the intrinsic interest of the life itself. It is sobering to note that *A Fortunate Life*, mentioned earlier, has been extremely successful with a fairly straightforward chronicle approach.

Most autobiographers seem to eschew either extreme and write somewhere between the two. That is, they employ a broadly chronological spine for the account of their lives, but gather events and comment in self-contained clusters along and within that chronology, occasionally moving back or forth in time.

Here, in note form, is autobiography that inclines towards the chronicle pole:

Age I7: Attempt to join up for World War I. Succeeded; but Ross, the farmer I worked for, told them my age. No hard feelings!

Age I8: Ross agreed to my enlisting, though he could have held me, farming being a reserved occupation. To Brisbane, where Wally was joining up too. Incident with Rebecca in train. [Break chronicle line to trace, through future, my correspondence with Rebecca till she died in Spanish influenza epidemic. Could have married her otherwise!]. The Recruiting Officer brawl. First camp. Drilling. On leave(s), Brisbane. Ted turns up, is able to join unit with Wally and me. The escapades of The Terrible Three.

To Sydney for embarkation.

Life on the troopship. Through the Panama Canal. New York. Introduced at theatre there as "brave Aztecs"!

Age I9: Further training on Salisbury Plain, Wiltshire. Biking around the villages. Knocking off sheep! West Country girls ... who said they didn't but sometimes they did!

The unit to France; but I get hospitalised by measles in Stroud! Wally survives the Somme battles but Ted MiA, believed dead.

To London for the Armistice.

To France, with the Army of Occupation. A champagne cache under a shell-damaged farmhouse. Billy Hughes visits the unit, promises us the world. [Break in chronicle again to trace, through immediate post-War period, the breaking-faith with this promise.] Injure my back lifting artillery pieces. [AUTHOR'S EXAMPLE]

And so on, through age 20, 21, 22 ...

Once the above were expanded into full text, it could comfortably comprise a chapter which might be titled "My War Service" or "For King and Country" or "War's Alarum" or "In Flanders Fields".

In contradistinction to this chronicle basis, material can also be organised in ways arising from the nature of the material itself and from links between items within it.

Such organising can result in crisscrossing from one time to another and from one place to another; and it is something other than Time or Place that brings the items together into chapter focus.

A straightforward example of gathering material around "themes" is to be found in Lord Goodman's *Tell Them I'm On My Way*, published by Chapmans in 1993.

Lord Goodman devotes a whole section to people he had known in the Arts world, in large part as a consequence of his posting as Chairman of the Arts Council from 1965.

There was for instance Francis Bacon, a well-known painter, in whose studio police claimed to have found drugs.

Lord Goodman, who intervened, was told by the inspector concerned that he was requesting Bacon to accompany him to Chelsea Police Station.

Here is Goodman's account:

> **"I am proposing," I said, "to tell Mr Bacon that he should not go anywhere with you." To which the inspector replied that if that were the case, he'd have to arrest him. "Please do," I declared, "and will you be good enough to tell me whether you have a notebook?" "Yes," sighed the inspector, "I have a notebook." "Good," I said. "Will you write down that at 9.10 a.m. you informed Lord Goodman that you were arresting his client, Mr Francis Bacon, and proposing to take him to a police station on the charge of being in possession of a substance which was a drug."**
>
> **"Would you also make a note that Lord Goodman rejoined that you were making this arrest before you had had any opportunity to examine the substance and that in his view the substance had been planted by the police."**

Such memoirs make good reading; and Lord Goodman writes with similar verve of Henry Moore the sculptor; Sir Laurence Olivier the actor; Peter Hall the producer; and several others like.

It is interesting that though these prominent figures would be fairly well known to those most likely to be reading *Tell Them I'm On My Way* the author still finds it worthwhile to supply character tags of a sort.

Henry Moore is presented pretty much as the quintessential gentleman: a delightful man, of firm character without any affectations, but quick in decision and as warm and reliable a friend as one could hope for.

This approximates a British ideal. In its romanticised form, the male who scores a stylish century at Lords before lunch, solves a murder or coolly foils a spy plot during the afternoon, and employs the evening to deliver a principled and witty speech in the House of Lords!

Sir Laurence Olivier emerges as heroic but of uncertain judgement; and Peter Hall as the admirable but flawed colossus — "a man of gigantic stature in theatrical terms, with some gigantic faults which are the faults inherent in a man of his stature".

If you have had interesting individuals in your life and can recreate them on the page, the theme of one chapter could well be about them?

Here is a somewhat lengthy example of organising material thematically; one that will repay careful analysis. It is from the magazine *Postmarks, Places And People* and is titled *Dornford Yates*. The author is Ken Forster.

Clearing out some personal correspondence going back forty years or so, I came across an item whose background story it may be interesting to account.

It is a somewhat timeworn and travel-stained Active Service Letter Card, hand-stamped at its point of origin, Salisbury, Southern Rhodesia [now Harare, Zimbabwe], with an indecipherable date, addressed to Lieut. R.K. Forster, RASC, No 1 GRTD, BNAF.

The front of the cover carries several redirection inscriptions, in manuscript, including one ... in indelible pencil, saying No 5 Section, Taranto, CMF, and the handscript date 21/5/44.

The letter card unfolds to reveal this message, conveyed in fairly clear handwriting beneath the date April 20, 1944.

"My dear Forster,

Your pleasant letter reached me after many days. It is very nice to know that my books have meant something to you and, particularly, that they have suggested that you should do likewise.

So many people can write, but don't, because they don't think they could. The converse is equally true. I envy you your admirable handwriting. It is so clear, yet takes so little room.

This war has hit so many people hard, and me among them. I have become a refugee: still, but for that, I might never have got back onto the Active List, so I have much to be thankful for.

I am no longer any good for anything but a staff job: but it is a great relief to be doing something. When I was sick and on sick leave, I went on with my writing: but I shall do no more until we have broken the Boche.

You have my very best wishes, and I thank you very much for writing me such a nice letter." The letter is signed, Yours sincerely, Dornford Yates.

For more than half a century novels under that pseudonym - the author's real name was Cecil William Mercer - have delighted, amused, angered, entertained, enchanted and infuriated many thousands of readers.

Dornford Yates was one of those novelists whose works one either loved or loathed.

His early titles included Berry and Co (1921), Jonah and Co (1922), And Five Were Foolish (1924) and they were followed by a series of romantic adventure stories (the 'Chandos' books) in the Anthony Hope idiom, under such titles as Blind Corner, Blood Royal and Fire Below.

His 34 Darnford Yates novels are a mixture of high adventure and lighthearted farce. Millions of copies were sold during his lifetime and many of his novels are still in print although some of his critics dismiss them as banal and snobbish. Be that as it may (a favourite Yates phrase) they were written with considerable skill and were said to combine the maximum of entertainment with the minimum of probability.

He died at his mountainside home at Umtali, then Southern Rhodesia, on March 5, 1960 at the age of seventy four.

It is difficult now, forty years on, to recall how and why I came to write to him, but I know that I did so c/o his London publisher during the closing years of 1943, when I was serving as the Camp Commandant of a General Reinforcement Training Depot with the British North African Force in Algeria.

I am sure, from his reply, that in the course of the letter I mentioned that I was planning to write a book or two when the war was over — in fact it was not till 1952 that my own first one was published — and I expect at the time that his letter encouraged me.

The war had dragged on from September 1939 and seemed, at this stage, as though it would go on forever, with all its attendant misery, heartache, separation and pain.

What I was not to know, wartime security being what it had to be, was that while I was writing to him from Algeria Dornford Yates was himself a serving soldier down in Southern Rhodesia.

So my letter, addressed to him in London, England, was re-directed to Salisbury, and his reply — this surviving memento — was sent to me in Algeria.

By the time it arrived there, in May 1944, I had moved on to Nola, near Naples, Italy. The Base Army Post Office people were not going to be beaten. They back-stamped the airmail form and channelled it after me, up to Nola.

But by now I was on the move again. I'd been posted to Southern Italy as a second-in-command of a Bulk Petroleum Storage Company in Taranto. It was here ... that Dornford Yates' letter, heavily endorsed and not a little travel-stained, eventually reached me ... a little over a month after it had been written.

I suppose this is all a rather inconsequential fragment of personal history. But one is bound, sometimes, to wonder how many items of written ephemera of this kind carry with

them untold stories of high hopes and heartaches, of small triumphs and of huge disasters in the lives and careers of the writer or of the recipient.

Dornford Yates, as I now know, had reached a watershed in his own private and public life about the time that he wrote this letter, as anyone patient enough to read his biography, published in recent years, could discover.

In my own less exalted sphere of life that period was also not uneventful.

In Naples, a few weeks earlier, I had applied for a job as a war correspondent observer at the Anzio bridgehead. My application had annoyed a certain fiery colonel and was refused because it had been made through the incorrect channel.

As a 'reprisal' for this piece of junior officer effrontery I was posted forthwith in a different capacity to a different destination — to Taranto and thence to Greece instead of to Anzio to almost certain obliteration

The officer who went to Anzio in my place was killed within forty eight hours of arriving there when his batman-driver, at the wheel of a Jeep, drove straight onto a German landmine.

Thus, is our destiny affected by many small matters. Had it not been for this turn of events the travel-worn airletter about which I am now writing would in all probability have carried one more terse endorsement.

It would, I suppose, have been marked "Killed in Action" and delivered in due course to my widow in England.

Having survived, now, for forty years I suppose this modest memento may some day find its way into a postal history auction or appear as a random item in a sale of literary ephemera.

If that is its ultimate fate I hope these few words may add to its interest, and to the pleasure of its eventual possessor.

This might seem at first to be indeed "a rather inconsequential fragment of personal history"; and of course it is, as it gets told to us, quite a simple little article.

It is in its organisation, though, more complex; moving back and forth as it does over some forty years and some half dozen locations in two continents. And it is quite a deal about the author's own life, though ostensibly about Dornford Yates.

Ken Forster takes as his starting point, his springboard, a "somewhat time-worn and travel-stained Active Service Letter Card" and traces this card's history from the circumstances that generated it to the thoughts it can still stir in him four decades later.

During this "journey" the author manages to communicate quite a deal about himself. He does this directly — his war service and his feelings about the war; his early interest in writing; his postmarks hobby. And also indirectly — from what he writes about the novelist Dornford Yates, he reveals a little more about himself too.

It is also worth noting:

- The piece has quite a distinct Beginning, Middle and End. That is, it is not random, unstructured, however casually it might in fact seem to move around. And while, finally, we probably reconstruct the events as chronicle in our own minds, it is not in fact written that way. Indeed, the account starts at the conclusion of the events being detailed; and thereafter, moves around within those forty years a good deal.
- It is an excellent example of how to take off from an old letter.
- There is some basic characterisation from actions, from talk (per letters), and even a little from beliefs and values — both for Ken Forster and Dornford Yates.
- The prose style is clear and unpretentious, which not only makes for easy reading and understanding, but also promotes our confidence in the narrator of the events, in his reliability and clear insights.

Such a couple of thousand words could well become part of a (thematic) chapter titled "Old Letters", or even "Strange Threads". Introduced perhaps thus:

> **Throughout my life there seems to have been groups of events that came together in ways defying all expectation and indeed likelihood. I was reminded of one of these when clearing out some personal correspondence going back forty odd years ... [AUTHOR'S EXAMPLE]**

The method Ken Forster has used can be applied more widely than just an incident within a chapter, however. Indeed, it can form the structural principle of a whole autobiography itself.

This is much the case with Richard Church's *Over The Bridge.*

In this work, Church manages to gather his entire young life around two images — an aquarium and a bridge.

It is an approach pretty much the opposite of *My War Service*, with its line of then, and then, and then.....

Church does, though, clearly consider his book as personal history. He subtitles it "An Essay in Autobiography"; and the very first sentences indicate he's dealing with what really happened.

We're given a genuine date, 1 January 1900; a real time — half past three in the afternoon; real places — Battersea and Chelsea in London; and real persons — two small boys who are brothers of seven and eleven.

> **It was the first day of January, 1900: New Year's Day; New Century's Day. But that portentous fact was of no interest to two little boys walking with extreme care and anxiety across Battersea Bridge at half past three in the afternoon.**
>
> **Their concern was immediate, for the elder brother, a small fellow of eleven, with a large nose, brown eyes, and a sallow skin that gave him a Spanish cast, was carrying an aquarium.**
>
> **This task so occupied him that his follower, the brother who shadowed his life ...**

And so on.

Church seems to realise that a straightforward Sunday-to-Monday account would be less than satisfactory hereon in his work. For one thing, no one can possibly remember all those Sundays-to-Mondays. They slip rapidly from the memory, blur and disappear. Church acknowledges this:

All that I recollect of that first day at school is …

Far from being daunted by this, though, the author simply launches into an attempted reconstruction of what he has actually lost to Time in this way.

Indeed, he will even have a go at recreating something of what he could never have experienced in the first place!

Here is his mother as, allegedly, his father first saw her:

He saw that (her eyes) were brown, shaded and troubled. He saw a thin face, with exquisitely moulded cheekbones touched with warm colour. He saw how her hair clustered softly over a pale forehead, whose serenity belied the trouble in the eyes below.

Church reveals no source for this information. Perhaps a photo? But even if so, that still wouldn't allow him to tap his father's consciousness at the point of the father first seeing Church's mother; which is what the passage attempts.

Perhaps his father told him of the moment, as indeed in later life his mother did tell him how she saw his father on that same first occasion? I would bet, though, that it's largely an imaginative reconstruction.

One might even accuse the author of being unacceptably cavalier with facts, as when:

My mother was nicknamed Roger Tichborne throughout the two or three years she spent at that College.

He hasn't bothered to find out whether she spent two years or three at "that College"; though it would surely have been easy enough to research.

Yet as already noted, the work also bristles with hard fact. For example — the historian Froude lived in the author's street. At Southampton, the boy Church was shown over that ill-fated vessel, the Deutschland. He was made captain of his school at Dulwich.

Clearly, then, we have an autobiography which, while centred on the writer's younger days and concerned to give accurate information about these in certain ways, is not attempting to provide standard chronicle.

So what *is* Church doing?

There can be no doubt that once we've read *Over The Bridge* we do know a great deal about the author's life and understand a good deal about it too.

The answer lies, to a considerable extent, with that "and understand" above. When you're reading a life, you don't want simply a Gargantuanly expanded *Who's Who* entry. You want also insights, illuminations. Equally, when writing this life, you want to explain and spotlight as well as to record.

And once you're into explaining, you get dragged right away from your time-lines. You start to take on board something of the weaponry of poetry — word pictures, vivid scene-setting, figurative language — imagery and metaphor. That is, what suggests and evokes as well as what states and declares. What is aimed at the heart, the emotions, as well as what is directed at the head, the intellect.

All these devices enable one to recreate a life on canvas, in colour, rather than a computer print-out. Though neither mode is to be despised — attempted re-creation, and straight record — as each conveys its own kind of truth.

The richest autobiographies are probably those where the one mode complements the other. As in *Over The Bridge*.

Let's proceed, then, to investigate what it is that Church is actually doing with this amalgam of, as it were, footprints and imaginative montage.

The chapter headings provide a good beginning. Nothing like "My War Service" or "School Days" or" We Build The Dam" or "Courtship With Kitti". But —

Ancestral Voices

Hornbook in Hand

Sunshine and Shadow

'Nature I loved'

And, of course, the final chapter, "Over the Bridge".

Such chapter heads indicate that the author isn't set to record his life in the order in which the days rolled out. Rather, he's grouping parts of it together because they seem to have particular associations one with another — themes.

For example, Chapter 9, "Irresistible Forces and Immovable Objects". This certainly doesn't deal with one separate part of Church's life when he came up against several irresistible forces and immovable objects, with the implication that before this point he'd never encountered any such and that after this encounter there were to be no more of them.

Rather, he moves back and forth over the span of youth-years telling, for example, how he discovered the wonderful world of boys' adventure stories and how intractable the real world seemed thereafter. He relates his brother's similar frustrating experiences during a phase of making mechanical toys which would never work properly; and even more dismaying and disruptive, the brother's desperate attempts to master piano playing.

The incidents illustrating the irresistible forces and immovable objects, then, are gathered in from several years and several areas.

Church himself explains something of the unifying principle of another of his chapters:

> **I have called the ... chapter "the influence of joy", and there could be no more accurate description of the full flood that flowed during those three years at Dulwich Hamlet School, carrying me so buoyantly. The keyword to that period of my boyhood is "recognition". I moved about in a widening universe and everything I saw, touched, smelled, every idea and mood, was new and burnished in its newness.**

Such a technique for dealing with dumb facts is equally evident in the first chapter, "The Aquarium".

The autobiography opens, as we've seen, with an account of two small boys very intent on conveying an aquarium over

Battersea Bridge. The narrative then pauses for several paragraphs to detail the provenance of this aquarium.

It is a gift from a neighbour, doubly valued by the boys because they'd so wanted such an aquarium; but their father was "so boyishly concerned with his own enthusiasms that he had ignored this longing", while their mother was "so apprehensive that she hesitated before committing herself, or her children, to the care of livestock".

Why, one might wonder, does the writer choose to begin this account of his life not with his birth but at age seven, and with the incident of the aquarium?

I suggest three reasons:

➢ This starting point allows the author to introduce what are to be the four major characters in this part of his life — himself, his brother Jack, his mother and his father. It also allows him to project the generally drab suburban setting, with its penny-pinching, parochialism and local bickerings — all very much part of his early years.
  Additionally, the two brothers are presented at an intense moment, when customary facades of behaviour are likely to be abandoned and underlying realities of character thereby revealed. The author actually spells out something of this:

  And how tense, how critical, was this particular moment! It marked a stage, a peak-point, in their lives. Both had longed, through childhood's infinity of time, for a gold fish. Their father, however ...

➢ It is a dramatic opening, one where there is action (mostly inner action) and conflict; rising tension; uncertainty as to outcome; and indeed, uncertainty too as to what had been happening before to give rise to these events.
  Such an opening engages the reader immediately. Not so a page of static information — "I was born at Battersea on March 26, 1893. My father was Thomas Church and he worked at the South West District Post Office ..."

➢ The third of the reasons, and the one most concerning this chapter, is the use of the incident as a kind of metaphor.

These events of the first chapter seem to image the whole autobiography itself.

That is ... the volume is a kind of aquarium.

The aquarium is a closed-in space, set apart, transparent, where a handful of creatures can be observed living out their lives in their own small and bounded environment.

So is autobiography. It too looks back to a closed-in space, of the Past. It is equally set apart, though by Time rather than by Distance. And it also allows a handful of creatures to be observed, living their lives in their own small and bounded environment.

Church even sees himself as rather like the afternoon sun in relation to the aquarium — it "threw a thwart beam ... into the aquarium and (lit) up its occupants, so that they shone like lighted ships".

That is, as sun is to aquarium, author is to book.

Here is the physical world of the boys' aquarium:

... [their] aim was to establish a real aquarium, with fresh waterscape scenery of strange, sodden greens, coralline grottoes, mosses, rondures, recesses, mournful weeds, sandy beds, pitted with glints of mica, animated with caddis-worms and molluscs; the silk-tinted water peopled not with one goldfish, but a number ranging in size, form, colour as various as a flight of Titania's fairies.

The following must then be the aquarium's correlative, autobiography?

Thus my realisation of the outside world was confined to a few streets around our little semi-detached house in the marshes of Battersea, between the famous park and the old parish church that stood out on a curve in the river. I seldom ventured as far as the park or the church; they were shadowy, foreign. A vague obscurity lay close about me much nearer home. I doubt if, at the age of seven years, my world was more than a quarter of a mile in radius, though I was frequently carried beyond that small area of light by my parents, the outer dimness being penetrated during such excursions by the all-light-beams of their divine authority.

Church speaks later of:

> **... my journey over the bridge of time into the past, and the setting up of a transparent theatre into whose fluid element I can stare at the living creatures evoked there, almost forgetting that I myself am one of them.**

Here the two terms, aquarium and autobiography, almost merge. Each is a transparent theatre of fluid element, lit by all-light-beams.

Here, too, the bridge metaphor is clear. It is a bridge into the Past.

Note how this is obliquely signalled in the first chapter:

> **... I remember still how I struggled with the conflict of emotions while we crossed the bridge.**
>
> **So we crossed the bridge; and at every passing of the horsebus, or a brewer's dray, the pavement trembled, the aquarium trembled, and we trembled.**

As the "real" aquarium had been fetched over the bridge by the two brothers, so Richard Church fetches back the aquarium of the past across the bridge of time.

This is quite a different way of organising one's material and writing up one's experience from that of *My War Service*.

What is reassuring is that both approaches, and especially the merging of both approaches, can make very effective autobiography.

Chapter Five

Peopling Your Life

Your life will not, you will no doubt have noticed, have been lived entirely alone, like Robinson Crusoe's before the arrival of Man Friday.

It has been inhabited by crowds of other human individuals; to say nothing of Dogs, Cats, Rabbits, Ferrets and Goldfish, as the *Sydney Morning Herald* used once to title one of the categories in its classifieds.

Many of these individuals were, and some will certainly continue to be, of first importance to you — because of great affection, or hostility, or simply because, irrespective of how you feel about them, they made some considerable impact on your life.

Any account of this life would, then, be incomplete and perhaps even incomprehensible without the inclusion of such characters.

How will you fetch them before your readers, then? So that they can be both visualised and understood.

This will depend considerably on the kind of work you are looking to produce. You might be content simply to add to the names, just information of a more or less statistical kind. As:

John Bellamy was an uncle by marriage to Beth, my mother's elder sister. There are certain inconsistencies regarding the date of his birth; but he certainly died in 1973, of lung cancer, at Richmond, Melbourne. He was an electrician of some sort, with his own small shop. He was

born in England, possibly at Stoke as he talked of his youth there; and emigrated as a young man. His death certificate states ... [AUTHOR'S EXAMPLE]

If you intend mainly to gather information for family record, the above would probably suffice, particularly as John Bellamy seems to have existed some distance out from the centre of your family circle anyway.

On the other hand, it could be that this uncle was a firm favourite, and very familiar and large-looming to you and yours. If so, then of course you'd want to know, and probably would already know, a good deal more about him. Indeed, if you were writing mainly for immediate family consumption, your readers would hardly need to be told much about him other than something of the facts outlined above. Any "picture" of him they can supply for themselves from their own experiences and recollections.

Of course, if you are hoping your autobiography will be read beyond family-and-close-friends, perhaps in published form, you'll need to create some "picture" of Uncle John. Players in the theatre of your life will be strangers to such readers, and you must recreate them.

No one is likely to want to read far if the Dramatis Personae are little more than names, dates and relationships.

Equally important, the nature of your interrelationships with these inhabitants of your life and world has to be made clear and comprehensible. Otherwise you, yourself, will emerge from your autobiography as similarly lacking in definition, as incomplete.

This takes us, then, somewhat into the area of fiction techniques — ways of characterising — that produce individuals both vivid and credible. You need only follow and employ these techniques as far as is commensurate with your particular purposes, of course. But however formal and non-literary a work you plan, vivid inhabitants can only enhance it, as record and also as reading matter.

For relatively minor characters, the so-called "tag" is usually sufficient. You look for something about the person that is striking, evocative and at the same time suggests that person as a whole, beyond just that particular "something", that tag, you've noted.

Often just a sentence or two will do this:

Aunt Matilda could sail into a room, with her majestic hat and imperious brolly, and sweep us silent with one slow survey.

Though Uncle Rupert was short and slight, he wore his glasses low on the bridge of his nose. At the dining table, his pale blue eyes could glimmer over the tops of steel rims ... and subdue us all entirely. [AUTHOR'S EXAMPLE]

This pair display similar *auctoritas* — and that's the tag. Though with Uncle Rupert, this isn't so immediately apparent.

To have established such characters thus, makes more credible your subsequent accounts of, say, trying to borrow money from either so that you and Elizabeth can buy your first home.

Aunt Matilda: "I do indeed approve of you and Elizabeth settling down and trust you will contribute offspring to the family. You may certainly have of me the sum required."

Uncle Rupert: "I'll consult my agent. In due course I'll let you know on what terms I might accommodate you."

[AUTHOR'S EXAMPLE]

It's worth noting that these two exchanges act to differentiate slightly the two characters. Each is still tagged *auctoritas*; but there's greater warmth and spontaneity underlying Aunt Matilda's.

Here are several lively and amusing character tags from Dickens, in whose works hundreds such abound.

This novelist simply presents one or two significant details, and there the minor character is, vivid as a Van Gogh portrait.

Here's a nurse self-effaced almost into extinction:

"Mrs ... ?"

"Blockitt, Sir?" suggested the nurse, a simpering piece of faded gentility, who did not presume to state her name as a fact, but merely offered it as a mild suggestion.

And Dr Blimber, who runs a school for young gentlemen:

Whenever a young gentleman was taken in hand by Dr Blimber, he might consider himself sure of a pretty tight squeeze. The Doctor only undertook the (education) of ten young gentlemen, but he had, always ready, a supply of learning for an hundred, on the lowest estimate; and it was at once the business and delight of his life to gorge the unhappy ten with it.

The awful Mrs Pipchin:

This celebrated Mrs Pipchin was a marvellous ill-favoured, ill-conditioned old lady, of a stooping figure, with a mottled face, like bad marble, a hook nose, and a hard grey eye, that looked as if it might have been hammered on an anvil without sustaining any injury. Forty years at least had elapsed since the Peruvian mines had been the death of Mr Pipchin; but his relict still wore black bombazeen, of such a lustreless, deep, dark, sombre shade, that gas itself couldn't light her up after dark, and her presence was a quencher to any number of candles. She was generally spoken of as a "great manager" of children; and the secret of her management was, to give them everything that they didn't like, and nothing that they did.

And Mrs Miff, a sort of vergeress, who (for a tip) will make sure you get one of the best seats in the church:

A vinegary face had Mrs Miff, and a mortified bonnet, and eke a thirsty soul for sixpences and shillings. Beckoning to stray people to come into the (church) pews, had given Mrs Miff an air of mystery; and there is a reservation in the eye of Mrs Miff, as always knowing of a softer seat, but having her suspicions of the fee. There is no such fact as Mr Miff, nor has there been, this twenty years, and Mrs Miff would rather not allude to him. He held some bad opinions, it would seem, about free seats; and though Mrs Miff hopes he may be gone upwards, she couldn't positive y undertake to say so.

Dickens is virtually inimitable, of course; and he tends to turn character into caricatures, which it is unlikely you'd be looking to do; but the underlying principles are pretty much those we've been discussing.

For those characters more central to your life, something more substantial that just a "tag" is required.

This presents no particularly difficult task. It's just one requiring observation, patience and a mastering of the appropriate techniques.

Even for primary characters, like your parents, your partner(s) and your children, you'd probably not be employing all the techniques to be examined shortly. You'd simply select those most likely to delineate the particular person.

For example, some of us are quite boldly outlined by what we wear; Bob(bie), for instance. Immaculate? Careless/casual? Very latest fashion? Grubby? Chic? Locked forever into Sixties garb?

On the other hand, it can be hard to recall what some people do in fact wear. Obviously it doesn't strike or indicate anything much of their character, which might itself suggest something about that character? Here are some of the techniques for capturing and rendering character:

- Dress
- Physical
- Appearance
- Actions
- Talk
- Values and beliefs
- Surroundings.

Dress

Certainly "clothes maketh the (wo)man"; and there is some sense in the quip that we are what we wear.

Here are two examples of fetching out a character largely through some detailing of the clothes he/she wears:

My mother decided that her 70th birthday would be an occasion for taking stock and initiating new directions. Her principle was — "I'm not going to be bullied any more by what people think. I'll do what I like. Anyone who isn't pleased — that's THEIR problem."

Translated into dress, this saw mother permanently panted, as it were. With elastic tops, for ease; dark colours, for not showing the dirt; and sloppy, for comfort. Accompanied by dark, somewhat oversized sweaters and shirts. Shoes with a message that heels had been banished forever.

For weeks at a time she'd don nothing but this Oldie Liberation uniform. All her floral, pleated frocks, with long sleeves to conceal her "scrawny arms", hung in her wardrobe in unregarded age. What she currently wore, lived in drawers.

This New-Age Old-Woman, relaxed and cheerful, pottered scruffily amongst us. [AUTHOR'S EXAMPLE]

This example takes the decision to change attitudes and lifestyle in a central character and shows how that decision manifested itself in terms of clothes — which in turn reveals much about my mother's gentle independence.

The next example is more narrative; but again, it uses dress to characterise:

Greg, I suppose, was my favourite nephew; but his mid-teens sorely tried our relationship.

He asked me once to accompany him on what amounted to an informal job interview with a businessman I'd had some amicable dealings with and who was prepared to give Greg a bit of weekend work. I felt happy enough about this ... till Greg turned up.

Hair full-blood Mohawk! Mercifully though, only the one colour. What looked like substantial key-rings dangling silver from one ear. Black leather jacket — in a Sydney February! Black sweatshirt beneath, emblazoning an obscure obscenity. Trousers, similarly escutcheoned, a blend of Western and Star Wars. The shoe designer had clearly found his inspiration in a nail punch.

Even the vocabulary of greeting ...

Fortunately, my business acquaintance was a sensible chap; and after a brief chat he simply said —

"This Saturday then. You'll need some old shorts, and a shirt, and tough boots. A hat wouldn't get too much in the way, either."

Greg, who still seemed able to recall some rudimentary English, agreed cheerfully. [AUTHOR'S EXAMPLE]

The above might suggest that each of your major characters has one particular and characteristic mode of dress only; and this could be misleading. John and Janet — to coin a couple — would dress quite differently in each of the following situations:

- At a wedding
- At a funeral
- At work — the office, the shop, on committee, cooking
- Gardening
- At the movies
- On a picnic.

It is likely, though, that something of John's or Janet's character would come through whatever they were wearing, anywhere; their conservativeness, or their extrovert nature, or their finicky traits, little-mindedness even; their lacking in self-esteem, eccentricity, extreme carelessness, etc.

Those of you who look to highlight a "people factor" in your life and who are prepared to put a deal of effort into doing this well, might work as follows:

1. List those you consider the main players. There won't, probably, be more than a half dozen.
2. For each of these, do a clothing inventory for the three or four situations where you'd be most likely to encounter them or where they show at their most characteristic. Playing tennis, for instance; or as above, cooking, gardening, at place of work, enjoying a red wine in front of a fire.
3. If any of these invite dramatising, rather than just an inventory of apparel, then put them into some little anecdote or even scene; preferably one that takes your "story"

forward at the same time, though the occasional pause or sidetrack can be successful too.

4. You should, at this point, have a number of completed pen-portraits through garments, dramatic or simply static. File these away. Some you will later be able just to slip into autobiography at some point, just as they stand. Others, you might use more as raw material — to remind you, or to feed fragments in.

Physical Appearance

This was to some extent covered under *Dress*, which is of course part of *Physical Appearance*.

As the examples there were longish, here are a few briefer ones of the kind you'd be using to establish some of the less important characters in your life:

My boss for some time after that was Bill O'Sullivan, a tall, shambling man with a black handlebar moustache. He looked as if he'd recently been discharged from the RAF and was just waiting around till a suitable pub came on the market somewhere civilised in the South of England.

Uncle Fred was stocky; short legs, solid as a full wheat bag, curly hair bleached as stubble, above a face as brown as his paddocks and eyes as faded a blue as the western skies.

[AUTHOR'S EXAMPLES]

Uncle Fred is a farmer — in nature as well as in occupation; and the description above attempts to suggest this as well as give an accurate description of physical appearance.

Little Nellie, at five, was sheer delight. Mostly freckles and grin. Shaggy hair surrounded her face, so that she peered out as if from under a disintegrating haystack. Matchstick legs, matchstick arms, and the appearance of a substantial apple concealed within each elbow and knee.

[AUTHOR'S EXAMPLE]

Actions

In a way this technique differs from those preceding in that it might be seen to require less skill. After all, don't people's actions simply speak for themselves? There is some skill, though, involved in the selection of actions to be recorded, and of course in setting these down clearly and, quite often, dramatically.

My wife folded the letter and replaced it in its envelope. She pondered. Then she looked up.

"I don't care what Emily's done," she said calmly. "I don't care any more about the things she's said. They no longer matter. She's in pain. She's desperate. She's ours. I'm going to her."

"Pack an overnight," I told her. "I'll get the car out."

[AUTHOR'S EXAMPLE]

This, of course, could equally well be offered as an example of *Talk* or *Values and Beliefs*, still to come. But the *Actions* within this frame of circumstances certainly suggest the kind of person my wife is.

Here's a different kind of *Actions*:

Wally wandered out into the garden, to wait.

He noticed the hose much tangled amongst the raspberry bushes.

He bent, drew it out, coiled it, hung it round the tap.

He walked on, gathering up several scattered stakes. These he stood against the lattice. He also pinched several laterals from the sole remaining tomato plant.

When Val eventually joined him, he was pondering a spade plunged in amongst withered onion tops. If not interrupted he would, without any doubt, have returned that implement to the garden shed ... where no one in our family would likely have ever dreamed of looking for it!

[AUTHOR'S EXAMPLE]

And another, different again:

Little survives to indicate what my great grandmother was really like. But something, perhaps, is suggested by the history of her will making-and-breaking over the last years of her life.

That of July 1887 had stood apparently for a decade and was pretty standard. Her beneficiaries were her children, in equal shares, her husband having predeceased her.

Then Richard, the youngest, must have played up, as he was omitted from the new will of March 1896. Right at this time, other records show, he had purchased the Green Ribbon Inn and also married Lucy Mant, lately from the North of England. There's no direct evidence of any link between these three near-contemporaneous events — Lucy, hotel and will; but still ... ? Three months after this an entirely new will appears. All now goes to Georgina [three quarter share] and The Benevolent Society.

There is no further change for fourteen months; then Georgina is disinherited completely. Now it's Annie and the Society, half share each.

Three weeks later, Georgina is just as inexplicably reinstated, almost the sole legatee now, with Annie left just a small sum, and the Benevolent Society perhaps feeling momently a good deal less benevolent.

There the will remained for the better part of a year; at which point great grandmother clinched it forever by departing to her (un)rest. [AUTHOR'S EXAMPLE]

It has never been clear to me from this will [o' the wisp?] whether I have a formidable old Matriarch screwing down tightly on her family, or a frightened old lady panicking from will to will; in both cases, with perhaps her old-age care in mind?

On balance, I'd go for the former. The sole extant photograph of her shows an upright and stern female in billowy black dress and severe black bonnet. She confronts the camera as if daring it to venture just one small impertinence. (Characterisation from dress here too?)

Do you know something of Wally from those actions in the garden? Does my wife convince as a real person? Have you a shrewd idea about my great grandmother? If so — with all these — then it's pretty considerably from the things they did and the way they did them.

Talk

By now you'll be getting the idea with these techniques. You'll yourself be able to work out something of how to use dialogue to reveal character. That is, what people say to each other indicating their personalities.

Two particular points, however, are worth making.

The first has to do with the whole question of reporting speech in any kind of "history", like autobiography.

It is extremely unlikely, even in this age of cassette recorders and such marvels, that you'll have much record of the billions of words you and those around you have exchanged over the course of your life.

So how on earth can you recall and reproduce accurately?

Well, of course you can't — not verbatim! And if that bothers you, as one who gives prime importance to accuracy, precision, the literal, then you'd best eschew attempting to incorporate direct dialogue into your work.

Some of you, though, will take the view that even if it's not possible completely to replicate past conversations, there's still value in getting down roughly how these went.

Literal truth might be lost; but a kind of general truth is tapped out and, we trust, conveyed.

My wife's words in response to Emily's letter, for example, cannot be exactly those I've attributed to her. Indeed, it was so distressing a situation that it's likely I only half-heard what she did, in fact, say. But I can guarantee I've caught both the spirit of the sentiments and the character of the speaker.

The second point has more to do with the craft of writing in general. Spoken words can be either *conversation* or *dialogue.*

There is a quite critical distinction.

Conversation is what we mostly *hear* around us. It might convey interesting and even vital information. It tends to be static rather than dramatic. It doesn't take you any further. At the end of conversation, you remain pretty much where you were when it began:

"Morning Bill. Nice enough sort of day?"

"Promises to be. You'll be out in the garden, I'd say?"

"Depends on the wife. She usually shops Thursday. But Grace is dropping by this week and can only manage the

Thursday, so we might have to shop this afternoon instead. How's Mavis?"

"Still got that damn virus. Can't throw it off. She's on antibiotics now. Affects her appetite. Milk upsets her. Has to miss out on the cornflakes. Complains about that."

"Confounded bug hit early this year. No one's had the vaccinations in time. Chap at the office down with it. We're all having to fill in."

"It's this long dry spell. They said so on the tele last night. Or it might have been the night before. It was when that doctor chap ... and he's always Wednesdays, isn't he?"

[AUTHOR'S EXAMPLE]

If you're still awake you'll realise what dreary stuff "conversation" is. Nothing has developed, progressed, from start to finish.

Compare with:

"Out!"

"This is my house too, Barney."

"Ten seconds!"

"And a writ served on you, I'm afraid. If you try ... "

[AUTHOR'S EXAMPLE]

Not a great many more than a dozen words here, yet the situation moves forward rapidly, from the first challenge to the response, to a third and then fourth stage of confrontation.

This is the sort of thing *dialogue* should do — *carry action forward* as well, of course, as offering revelation of character — which is the context in which it is being discussed here. (Two very definite and strong characters; yet the second speaker is a calmer person than the first; less angry? Which we pick up simply from the words they speak.)

If you look back to the Emily-letter sketch, you'll note that there, too, the exchange of words acts to carry events forward.

The passage moves from being presented with a situation to making a decision about it — to having that decision endorsed and entering into realisation, action.

If you are unhappy about writing dialogue because of its fiction element, a good compromise is to use indirect speech, reported speech. This way, you convey pretty much what was said on the occasion, but you don't make any claim to be giving a verbatim reproduction.

When a January mail brought me my first teaching appointment, I was mightily dashed. It seemed so remote a location that I remarked that it would probably require a two day train journey then a switch to camel!

My father, however, quietly pointed out that although I'd be living far from the family and friends and metropolitan life that was all I'd known, I had been given this opportunity to take education to kids who knew little of life beyond their far-flung farmhouses. He made clear what I'd find myself representing within that outback community; and clear, too, what I could learn myself from such a three year stint; what might enrich my own life in the course of the task.

[AUTHOR'S EXAMPLE]

Reporting speech in this way gives the essentials of what I'd said as well as my father's more ample comment. Yet no one could object that it's pretending to be what is manifestly isn't — "exact words".

Values and Beliefs

A statement of these also acts to construct and register character.

The range of possibilities is wide:

- *You can simply establish for a character a sort of general attitude to life.* May is earnest, or mischievous, or timid. Peter is aggressive, or sports mad, or moths fly out of his wallet.
- *You can link a character to some specific ideal.* Tom is a fervent "family man". The sanctity of the home is central to his life and probably even determines his vote at elections.
- *You can link a character to a particular ideology.* Mariellen is the quintessential feminist — or leftie — or greenie — or indeed all three!

- *You can link a character to some crusade more narrowly "moral".* Old Uncle William is fiercely anti-gay — or thunders against unmarried mothers. Whereas old Uncle Ponty (whom I greatly prefer) takes head on the tobacco companies and their advertising.

This sort of tagging is, of course, more suitable for the less prominent people in your life. It sums them up in ways that draw attention not only to what they're like, but to their main influence on you and role with you.

For those more important to your life, more complex characterisation is required, to reflect the greater complexity of the relationship. You would, probably, be looking to employ a whole range of these techniques.

I went with Johnno to the RSL that evening. They were doing Birthday Calls, in between spots.

Johnno listened to a couple. Then —

"Actually it's Karl Marx's birthday. Today."

I returned his grin. Johnno composed his craggy features, strode purposefully up to the bow-tied compere. A few words. Then over the PA system —

"Spell it with a C or a K? How old did you say ... ?"

Fortunately the band struck up at this awkward point, with "Happy Birth ...day ... " And thus it was that that bastion of political conservatism, all enthusiastic and innocent, hymned Birthday Homage to the Great Red Monster himself!

[AUTHOR'S EXAMPLE]

And thus also is the mischievous and politically well informed character of my friend Johnno firmly established.

More straightforwardly — if you were to trace the steps by which your brother or your sister came to be religious, you'd not only be recording facts that meshed in with those of your own life, you'd as well be projecting much of that sibling's character, through the *Values and Beliefs* underlying their religious ambition and vocation and its realisation of these.

Differently again — my niece Sue. I would introduce her by an account of her trek around banks, aged about fifteen, demanding a non-interest bearing account on the grounds that interest charging is morally indefensible and socially irresponsible.

She has now, almost two decades later, reconciled herself to some moderate usurious return on her capital. She has also worked herself into being one of the nation's top credit and consumer law specialists; has been influential in significant Federal Government reforms in these areas; and has ridden Lone Ranger-of-all-Time against those financial institutions that prey on the unwary and the vulnerable.

Her adolescent crusade, then, encapsulated an ideal and a drive that set directions for much of her life. It certainly would illuminate for the reader *Values* that are quite central to Sue's character.

The presentation of Sue in this way, incidentally, makes interesting contrast with the son of a friend who, in his middle teens or so, began castigating his parents for "sordid materialism" — in the main, because they'd invested in a pair of semis against their old age. He was still rumbling the same line when, a few years later, he'd moved into one of the semis while doing a degree — rent free, of course!

Surroundings

Once more, possibilities range widely.

For example, you could well have relatives and friends who are at least to some extent characterised by their "space". In particular, rooms that are more personally theirs.

You will be able to distil a character from this room:

Floor: Pale blue wall-to-wall, with tiny dark-blue flecks.

Walls: Papered, ivory with small posies of roses yellow and red.

Window: Bay, white wood, small panes. Filmy, pale blue curtains.

Furnishings: Very soft bed with pale blue quilt. Fringed ivory pillow covers. Antique dresser, oval mirrors, ornate

drawer handles. Jars and glass bowls of pale blue. Victorian basin and jug, flowered.

The inhabitant above could never be confused with the next inhabitant below:

Floor: Polished boards, dark. Rust-coloured rugs, both shaggy and well worn. A small, Turkish-looking rug with a few dog hairs attached.

Walls: Timber panelling, scratched and faded in parts.

Window: French doors leading onto a paved terrace, then old garden. (Leaves need sweeping.) Brass handles. Casement window in opposite wall, of timber.

Furnishings: Two leather settees, somewhat out of shape, with old and non-matching cushions and a copy of *Fiction Review*. Timber walking-stick stand inside the door. Timber desk and chair, the former showing ink and mug stains. Papers, envelopes, pens and the like scattered over it, with two heaps of books, places tagged in them with paper slips. Also a dog lead, tangled; and several packets of vegetable seeds.

One room belongs to grand-aunt Lucille and the other to old Uncle Ferguson, recently retired from an English Literature Department. One could hardly mistake whose room is whose!

Rooms, however, are only one of the *Surroundings* our autobiography characters inhabit. Other possibilities include:

Workplaces: Garden Shed. Neatly stacked shelves, implements hanging from brackets, tagged drawers?

OR ... just heaps of garden things stacked all over the floor and stuffed onto shelves.

Office:

Kitchen:

Garage:

Car: Basic model, battered, litter-filled?

Glittering, all accessories, oversized tyres?

Tiny: "The crazy way he drives it, it's like being flung around inside a tin can!"

Golden-fleece seat covers, Aztec trinkets dangling, stickers from all over the US ...

Try yourself out. Do you have a character who would put on a small party? If so, itemise several of the rooms concerned (kitchen, lounge, front verandah) as he/she would set them up. For example, are the nibbles likely to be seaweed rice pieces, or cubes of supermarket New Zealand tasty with Jatz crackers?

Or, the kind of holiday one of your major characters used to take; the luggage, inside and out; the clothing worn; the means of travel; the degree of organisation (if any!); the venue.

File both away.

You will likely use them, or parts of them, hereafter. There are, no doubt, other ways in which a lively author can transmit to readers real, living and engaging characters; but those above seem the basic ones.

In autobiography, of course, you are limited in a way that fiction isn't, in that you are not inventing character to suit an authorial purpose.

Your people already exist, many of them in your present world and others, of course, in your memory or through report. Your task is to transfer these "real" people to your pages in such a way that your readers can see them, that they become more than just names with a few statistics attached.

To do this well is in turn to rerun your own life much nearer to the way it has truly been. The feel and colour and temperature of it, as well as the facts and outlines. The way it all seemed at the time. This will also make your autobiography a more interesting experience for those who pay you the compliment of choosing to read it.

One final and possibly reassuring point.

I have throughout these sections supplied many of my own examples of the techniques of characterisation. These necessarily reflect my own style and tone, which are very often of the keeping-it-light kind, with an occasional dash of near-melodrama; and a little "literary", perhaps, from my professional background.

This certainly does not mean that you must try to do it this way. Quite otherwise! You have your own voice and you must stay with that or your whole account is likely to ring false. This, in turn, would undermine your work as an honest statement of your life and your world.

Albert Facey's writing style is pretty much his character and indeed his life; they strike exactly the same note. I certainly wouldn't attempt to write the way he does. As, quintessentially, in the final lines:

> **The following year my wife became very ill and she was sent to hospital several times, for weeks at a time. I engaged several different doctors but she never got much better. She seemed to get worse as the years went by and she had several blackouts. Then, on the eighth of July 1976, she became unconscious and stayed in that state until the third of August 1976. She died at seven o'clock at night in my arms. We had been married for fifty-nine years, eleven months and twelve days. So on this day the loveliest and most beautiful woman left me.**
>
> **Evelyn had changed my life. I have had two lives, miles apart. Before we married I was on my own. It was a lonely, solitary life — Evelyn changed that. After our marriage my life became something which was much more than just me.**
>
> **I now wish to end this story. On the thirty-first of August 1977, I will be eighty-three years old — another birthday. The loss of my lovely girl, my wife, has been a terrible shock to me.**
>
> **I have lived a very good life, it has been very rich and full. I have been very fortunate and I am thrilled by it when I look back.**

To complement "my" examples and those of other writers I have chosen, go out to your own reading of fiction/biography/autobiography and see how these authors block out their characters, real or imagined.

Indeed, this is by far the best way to pick up and hone any of the writing skills: go see how others do it — and improve upon these!

Here's Virginia Woolf doing a cameo on her parents — fictionalised, but that's who the couple are. She takes as theme one particular area of the relationship — the daily life together. Note how many of our characterising devices she employs.

> **But it would be a mistake, she thought, thinking how they walked off together, she in her green shawl, he with his tie flying, arm in arm, past the greenhouse, to simplify their relationship. It was no monotony of bliss — she with her impulses and quicknesses; he with his shudders and glooms. Oh no. The bedroom door would slam violently early in the morning. He would start from the table in a temper. He would whizz his plate through the window. Then all through the house there would be a sense of doors slamming and blinds fluttering as if a gusty wind were blowing and people scudded about trying in a hasty way to fasten hatches and make things ship-shape. ... all because [father], finding an earwig in his milk at breakfast had sent the whole thing flying through the air onto the terrace outside. ... Other people might find centipedes. But he had built round him such a fence of sanctity, and occupied the space with such a demeanour of majesty that an earwig in his milk was a monster.**
>
> **But it tired [mother], it cowed her a little — the plates whizzing and the doors slamming. And there would fall between them sometimes long rigid silences, when ... half plaintive, half resentful ... she brooded and sat silent. After a time he would hang stealthily about the places where she was — roaming under the window where she sat writing letters or talking, for she would take care to be busy when he passed, and evade him, and pretend not to see him. Then he would turn smooth as silk, affable, urbane, and try to win her so. Still she would hold off ... would turn her head ... At length, standing outside the group the very figure of a famished wolfhound he would say her name, once only, for all the world like a wolf barking in the snow but still she held back; and he would say it once more, and this time something in the tone would rouse her, and she would go to him, leaving them all ... and they would walk off together among the pear trees, the cabbages, and the raspberry beds. They would have it out together ... until it was time for dinner, and there they were, he at one end of the table, she at the other, as usual.**

This couple have become two of the best known and most vividly realised characters of twentieth century literature.

We can now understand rather better why this is so? And the skills involved, together with the confidence engendered, will allow us to attempt to recreate for our readers even those folk who inhabited days before our own.

Which is what the next chapter tells of.

Chapter Six

Those Carved Names

Down their carved names the raindrop ploughs
From Thomas Hardy's poem
During Wind and Rain

This chapter is for autobiographers who look to include in their work some account of their ancestry: of those who lived before us, have done their best and worst, and departed.

Many of you will be planning no more than a few pages of family history. Your attention will be directed rather to your own years and happenings; and the likelihood is you'll have neither the impulse nor the skills to be undertaking extensive genealogical researches.

Those who, on the other hand, want to work this family history vein quite extensively could seek guidance beyond this relatively brief section from, say, Nancy Gray's *Compiling Your Family History* or *Roots And Branches: Ancestry For Australians*, by Errol Lea-Scarlett. Local libraries would almost certainly have other such titles available. This chapter in our text here sets out to give a basic introduction to researching ancestry and some guidance in writing up the results into autobiography.

It can, indeed, add quite a lot to an account of one's life to have a section detailing something of those folk in funny coats and hats who bequeathed to us so much of what we are.

Those who are ours, though we never knew them. They are not even memory; just a handful of dry facts and elusive reputation to rattle around our imaginations.

What you do manage to turn up, though, will almost certainly be of considerable interest and could have an impact quite unexpected.

For example — Elizabeth's ancestors, she discovered through research, came to Australia last century on a ship where fever raged. The dead were consigned in daily ceremony to the deep. When sharks followed and ravaged the corpses, in full view of horrified survivors, the consigning ritual was switched to night.

Two boys, Ralph (12) and Jack (10) saw both their parents and their one sibling, a sister, so cast from them forever. They had aboard no other relatives.

There seems no record of what happened to those boys when the vessel finally berthed at Melbourne. Presumably someone amongst the passengers or ship's company got them ashore and perhaps even took them in.

There appears, likewise, no record of where or with whom they lived until a decade later they emerged as independent and presentable adults.

These mysterious and so admirable great-greats have bequeathed Elizabeth, she feels, an enormous sense of pride in her origins. What those battered and abandoned youngsters confronted, endured and surmounted, she tells, wonderfully extended her own emotional and spiritual boundaries.

Equally heart-rending, though without any accompanying heart-warming component, was the unearthing of the Mary Randall story.

Mary was tried in 1791, found guilty of receiving stolen goods and sent to New South Wales for fourteen years.

She seems to have had seven children, with Polly the eldest and a "young Mary". Yet she arrived in Sydney with only year-old Sarah.

The others? Presumably, they were enforcedly abandoned to the cold and hunger of London's harsh East End.

Thus our forebears — uncertain outlines stalking the centuries. Almost unknowable now, for the most part, yet linked to us forever by those primary bonds of blood and destiny.

Let's search them out.

General Names

These can suggest both occupations and locations.

Let's take Armstrong, for instance — my wife's maiden name.

This has strong associations with the Scottish Borders. Centuries back, Armstrongs would raid into England for cattle and other plunder. Armstrong has become something of a regional name.

Others have origin in occupations — Wheelwright, Cartwright, Smith, Turner, Driver, Tanner, Weaver, Baker, Miller, etc.

If your name were Fowler now you could be wondering whether there was any link with English East Anglia, particularly with the Fenlands, as fowling was for centuries a common occupation thereabouts.

Names, in themselves, seldom provide hard fact; but in conjunction with other information, with hints and family legends they can lead you to areas of further search; open up possibilities.

One of my great-greats was a George Lepherd, (also Lephard, Leopard, Lepperd and Lepard). Such a variety of spellings would suggest either illiteracy (which other sources in fact support); or the Anglicising of an European name; or indeed both.

This Anglicising possibility opens up when you discover that Lepherd came from Wandsworth, in London, where in the nineteenth century lived quite a population of Jewish refugees from pogroms in Eastern Europe, particularly from Poland.

Might he then, with such a name, have been Jewish? Certainly both his mother and his first child were named Rebecca.

And adding a little to this possibility is the fact that of all her generation only Aunt Alice railed against Grandfather Lepherd ("that parasite...!") and Aunt Alice was scandalously anti-Semitic.

So? Only circumstantial, of course, but enough there, I'd think, to set one on a fishing expedition amongst Jewish and refugee/immigrant records and the like.

For publications about general names, and researchers skilled in this area, look through genealogical journals like *Descent*, published by the Society of Australian Genealogists at Richmond Villa, 120 Kent Street, Sydney 2000.

General names, however, are unlikely to get you very far very often. Spellings change, occupations change, people move about, women take on married names.

When my wife checked her Armstrongs back to the eighteenth century, not one turned up anywhere near those Borders. Many, in fact, collected by that other border in the United Kingdom — the Welsh Marches. And the males proved all perfectly respectable middle class doctors and lawyers, with women of standing — nary a cattle-raider amongst them!

Your major activity in this ancestor search will be directed towards unearthing whatever documentary information, as opposed to conjecture, exists about them.

The first steps will possibly already have been taken to some extent, out of earlier chapters here. That is, you will have noted whatever family "facts" you have access to or can reliably remember, about your parents, grandparents, aunts and uncles.

These would include dates of birth and death, of marriage and of any other events of consequence.

Look to Family Bible entries, if such exist, to expand and confirm these. Take care, though, with those that pre-date the volume's publication, as these will likely have been entered from memory or some other and unverifiable record.

Note down, too, details of residences for parents, grandparents, etc. and places of education, occupations, names and details of their children, and the like. Also look out for anything readily accessible from certificates, records of professional qualifications, prayer books, parish newspapers, school prizes, postcard and photo collections, scrap books, school magazines and reports, birthday books.

Later, of course, you'll be looking at such items to yield heaps of general speculation; but for the moment, just facts, mostly dates and names.

Note, perhaps by circling in red, any dates or whatever that are even slightly suspect. This will prevent you from forgetting the circumstance and later heading into error. Also, if further on you run into inconsistencies with dates, as often happens, you'll know where the error is most likely to be and check around there first.

For example, my wife was perplexed by dates seeming to indicate that her great grandfather had married Elizabeth Sommerville twice! The mystery deepened when grave stones in Wales showed that in between the two weddings Elizabeth Sommerville had also managed to fit in dying and getting buried!

Further (fascinated) investigations revealed that there were in fact two Elizabeth Sommervilles, almost certainly cousins. And that my wife's grandfather believed in wasting no time between ceremonies.

When you've collated all known facts and dates, it's time to start researching — backwards from now.

Certificates

Get a copy of your own birth certificate (if you don't already have one: you require it these days for passports and the like), and add to your file any new material from that.

You might find, for instance, that your father gives his full name as Patrick Dingle Jones; and that the "Dingle" is quite new to you. It would not be difficult to suggest a reason for this suppression of "Dingle"; yet you might need to know the full name for application to gain access to other material.

Next, gather your parents' marriage certificates and birth certificates, and of course death certificates if they are no longer living. Then from them to your grandparents' certificates; and then their parents.

You'll find the amount of information getting progressively less the further you go back. On the other hand, the proportion of new information will be increasing; about occupations, for instance, and cause of death.

Even the witness section on an older marriage certificate proved of considerable interest to me when I turned it up. This role had been performed by a particularly prominent and highly regarded citizen. When one considers that the bride was the daughter of two convicts, both present at the ceremony, one can draw inference that the family had indeed won firm status of respectability.

Witnesses can turn out to be family members too, and hence provide starting points for other sorties into your past as you go after their scripts.

Anyway, continue this procedure of going back through certificates, using the information on one to make applications for the others, until you reach those generations first arriving in Australia. After that, you'll need to tap into overseas records — of which more later.

It is worth noting that marriage certificates tend to be the most reliable as the details are supplied by those most closely connected with the event. Also, death certificates sometimes give information not readily available elsewhere, as number-of-years-in-the-colony from which if necessary approximate arrival dates can be calculated. Also, the town or parish where born in the UK, which can be the springboard for overseas researches.

This sending for certificates is a quite straightforward procedure, but it can also prove an expensive one. You simply check with the authorities listed below about how you should apply, and the fees required.

Registry of Births, Deaths and Marriages, PO Box 30, GPO, Sydney 2001.

Registry of Births, Deaths and Marriages, GPO Box 4332, Melbourne 3001.

The Registrar-General, PO Box 118, Albert Street, Brisbane 4002 (for post 1890); OR The Queensland State Archives, PO Box 1397, Sunnybank Hills, 4109 (for pre 1890).

The Principal Registrar, GPO Box 1351, Adelaide 5000.

The Registrar General, PO Box 7720, Cloisters Square, Perth 6000.

The Registrar General, GPO Box 198, Hobart 7001.

The Registrar, Births, Deaths and Marriages, GPO Box 788, Canberra, ACT 2601.

The Registrar General's Office, GPO Box 3021, Darwin 0801.

(*For information about certificated material from outside Australia, you had best refer to one of the more substantial genealogical guides. You'd need to know, for example, that in France, births etc. are registered and held in local areas rather than in provincial or national centres. You'd also need to know some French!)*

Texts on compiling family history will offer you quite complex systems for transferring and recording all this information — genealogical tables and trees and the like. These are fine and worth mastering if your project is solidly genealogical rather than primarily autobiographical.

I have found it entirely adequate, for opening stages at least, simply to use the methods outlined earlier. That is, name on top of a sheet, followed by items of information.

Such a sheet can at appropriate times be reorganised, putting items in chronological order, say, or under particular heads, as *Relationships, Education and Career, War Service.*

The main names might even expand into a folder each.

Once this has all been done — and the gathering can take many months, with all the postal to-ing and fro-ing, to say nothing of wrong certificates turning up as a result of name changes and uncertainties about which State, second marriages and the like — once all this has been done, you can either write it up immediately or wait until you've tapped the much less secure area of memories.

About those difficulties that can be encountered, as noted in the paragraph above: I could never locate a birth certificate for my maternal grandfather, Peter Purcell. I had the date and place; but the Registrar General was adamant there was no record.

Then a relative pointed out that we'd had a cousin who'd died young — Pierre. I'd always wondered how such a French name had entered this very Irish and Welsh family and I suddenly saw that I could have a source if still not altogether a reason.

I tried Peter Purcell's date and place with Pierre Purcell and up it came!

It is perhaps worth noting that information missing from government records can occasionally be found in church Registers of Baptisms, Marriages and Burials. This is becoming much less likely, though, as over late decades such material has been increasingly transferred to central civil records.

You'll now have basic information about your forebears. This could include full names; dates of births, marriages and deaths, causes of deaths; parents and spouses and children and siblings; places of births, marriages and deaths; occupations; and possibly other items.

There are a number of other sources you can tap to add to all this, to the extent that you wish to take your researching further.

Here they are.

Inquests

These are enquiries, before a coroner, into a death occasioned by violence or where the death is unexplained in any satisfactory way.

Hence few deaths call for an inquest; but where one does, its record will often be rich in material and fascination. Here is an edited record of the inquest held at the Black Horse Inn, Richmond, on 7 May 1822. Margaret Randall, daughter of convicts Paul and Mary Randall, had recently married surgeon and convict Henry Francis Seymour and the couple had taken over the inn.

One Fanny Pentony had been found dead on the inn floor.

Thomas (Skinner) gave evidence that he had met Fanny and invited her to "a glass of spirits" and "she replied yes and thank you". So he took her to "Paul Randall's Public House". He could not recollect what spirits they had asked for except that it included both brandy and gin, because "he was not sober himself when he brought the deceased into the public house".

Thomas was, however, able to recall that "he laid down drunk in the tap room and the deceased lay upon him with her head upon his thighs and in that position she was found dead". He'd discovered this, he explained, when a servant John Egleton arrived, and "another person of the common appellation of Black Joe".

Egleton told the inquest how he was awakened by shuffling noises, went to the taproom and found Black Joe crouched over the couple on the floor.

He asked "What are you doing to those persons asleep?" Black Joe explained that:

> **Seeing a woman laying in the same room drunk he wished to have a connection with her and said he would. He then told the servant John Egleton that this was his intention and Egleton told him he should not but he persisted in endeavouring to complete his purpose.**
>
> **He approached the deceased and found the man upon whom she laid making a noise and he desisted for a short time and then he went a second time and found her thighs cold and says to the servant Egleton, she won't do, she is cold, she is dead — then he says Egleton alarmed the house and Mr Seymour got up and said she was defunct.**

Margaret Randall estimated that the couple had consumed in excess of two pints of brandy each — a state of "perfect intoxication" — so it is hardly surprising that the good men of the county determined that Fanny Pentony came to her death by this means aforesaid and not otherwise!

It is impossible to overestimate the value to an autobiographer of such a document, recreating so vividly and in such detail the daily world of one's ancestors; even if occasional, somewhat gross, fragments, do appear.

Wills

The Supreme Court in each State keeps records of deceased estates — which for our purposes, means for the most part wills. Sometimes instead of a will there's a Document of Administration.

Wills, as you might expect, vary from the utterly formal and colourless to those charged with technicolour drama.

Here are a few sections from Margaret Seymour's will. They hold a number of small but illuminating items of interest which you could weave into your account of your ancestors. It is dated 14th July, 1875, some three months before her death.

> **THIS IS THE LAST WILL AND TESTAMENT of me MARGARET SEYMOUR of Richmond in the County of Cumberland and Colony of New South Wales Innkeeper and widow and relict of Henry Francis Seymour late of Richmond aforesaid surgeon deceased. I direct that my Executors herein after named shall cause my body at my decease to be placed in a leaden coffin and deposited beside the remains of my said dear departed husband in the vault at the burial ground attached to St Peter's Church Richmond aforesaid. And it is my express desire that after my burial as aforesaid the said vault shall be thoroughly closed up and never afterwards reopened on any pretence whatever except for purposes of repairs. I also direct that my said vault shall be kept in repair as hereinafter provided.**

The "said vault" remains yet in the cemetery opposite St Peter's Church of England, Richmond, though no longer noticeably "in repair". The will then details numerous legacies, many to "old servants"; and finishes with an important item for descendants of Sophia Sly:

> **All other real estate of which I shall die possessed I give devise and bequeath to and to the use of Sophia Sly widow of William Sly, Senior, deceased, her heirs executors**

administrators and assigns absolutely — in consideration of her long and faithful services and her unremitting kindness to me during a period of forty years, and trusting to her wise discretion as to how she shall use and dispose of the same, and upon consideration, nevertheless, of and charged and chargable with the continual keeping in repair the vault and tomb in which my remains shall be deposited as aforesaid at an annual expenditure by the said Sophia Sly or her representative of not less than three pounds and three shillings.

An example of the important leads that can be turned up in a will occurs in Anne Lepherd's (nee Jones). This was inserted mid-page, in crabbed handwriting:

In the event of all my grandchildren dying before attaining twenty one years of age I devise all my property to my brother Daniel Rees and my sisters Gwen Rees and Anna Rees absolutely equally to be divided between them.

This insertion, with the accompanying margin addresses, provides now the sole link back to nineteenth century Wales.

You will now be familiar, if you were not so already, with the way to write up formal documents in human terms. It could be a good idea here to allow yourself two sheets or folders for each will, one for the facts themselves, the other for your extrapolations from these — what you read into them. The integrity of your autobiography depends quite a deal on keeping and acknowledging distinction between fact and speculation.

If Death Duty has been involved with the estate, it would be worth pursuing the Death Duty File, which sometimes contains additional information.

So too might the documentary file, if one exists. It would hold the original of the will, with perhaps additions and alterations, and household or other inventories. The Affidavit of Executor/Administrator File can also turn up interesting personal information.

You can apply for copies of wills to the Registrar of Probate, Supreme Court, City, State. Genealogical Societies often hold transcripts of wills, with indexes, so it could be easier to try there first.

Wills on occasions contain information about other members of the family and about property. Margaret Randall's will, for instance, makes apparent that Sophia, to whom is bequeathed the Black Horse Hotel, must be an adopted child. As there were virtually no adoption records that century, that item of information is particularly valuable.

This same will lists all the property the Seymours owned in Richmond in 1875 — that could be a chore to track down any other way.

Land Records

This is more involved as there are several title systems in Australia and not all records are readily accessible. It is worth pursuing, particularly with "old title", usually held in packages with Registrar Generals or equivalent. All sorts of unexpected statements and evidences can drop out from these.

Useful for those few who have "landed ancestors" would be the application forms for land, deeds of grant and conveyance, and the like. Check with archives/libraries in each State for sources of these.

Take information about these latter, though, with the customary caution as they might contain "facts" about character that are less than fully disinterested! Nice guys get grants, you see, or dubious title confirmed. So character can be spruced up for an occasion.

Here is "The Respectful Memorial of Paul Randall" to Governor Macquarie, dated 5th March 1821. Its frame and purpose will be self-evident:

To His Excellency Governor Macquarie.

The respectful memorial of Paul Randall, humbly herewith.

That Your Excellency was pleased to grant Memorialist an allotment of acres of Land in the Town of Richmond.

That memorialist has built a house upon the said allotment and completed it in a manner much superior to Your

Excellency's General Order and Instructions on that Head; and in consequence of the advanced age of himself and wife, Memorialist humbly and anxiously begs to obtain the deeds of the said allotment of land, in order for the more permanent security of the said land and premises to his daughter and only child, to whom he will bequeath it, God willing.

That Memorialist with all humility and the greatest deference submits this memorial to Your Excellency's benign consideration and craves your Excellency's gracious sanction to its humble petition. And as in duty bound will ever ...

This somewhat self-abasing exercise was successful, in that the property did indeed pass on to daughter Margaret; wife of Henry Francis Seymour, convict and surgeon, and in due course proprietor of the Black Horse Inn.

Shipping Lists

This term is usually used in connection with free settlers, though of course such lists existed for convicts too. Indeed, the latter at times are much the more informative lists.

Some ships, particularly in the later nineteenth century, drew up a list of all passengers, sometimes with the addition of information like occupation. Other lists simply named the VIPs or higher fare passengers, dismissing the remainder with the like of "and 47 steerage" or "30 persons, servants and others".

Such records have often been preserved by shipping and/or harbour authorities, and can be consulted in archives and libraries.

There were also lists under *Shipping Intelligence* in the newspapers of the first quarter of the nineteenth century. You will find reproductions of such lists in *The Historical Records of New South Wales* and *Historical Records of Australia.*

Those arriving on "bounty" ships tend to be particularly well documented, with details including often the educational standard of the assisted immigrant; so do seek out such lists as appropriate; and entitlement certificates and the few disposal lists.

The New South Wales State Archives holds the above kinds of materials; sometimes for beyond that State's borders too. Its *Concise Guide* is almost indispensable for such searchings.

More and more, too, area and specialist libraries are holding selected copies of such records; so it's worth a try locally as a first move.

Cemetaries

Armed with names and areas of residence, you can simply wander up and down aisles and see what you stumble across.

This worked very well for me at Richmond, NSW. Three times I was led by a name I knew to one I didn't and ultimately to a couple of families who were linked to the Black Horse Inn but about whom I'd known nothing. Living members of these families who'd been doing their own genealogy were happy to offer me fruits of their researches and I was able to exchange with them mine.

More sensibly, though, you could approach the adjoining church or the local authority for information from Burial Records and the like.

Waverley Council in Sydney, for example, is through its library very helpful. Much information about its cemetery's "inhabitants" has already been abstracted and recorded. Cemetery walks are conducted throughout the year.

Other groups have recorded headstone inscriptions and will make these available — indeed, they will often have been published. This, naturally, is particularly valuable — indispensable! — for cemeteries which have now disappeared. Genealogical Societies can tell you who and where for such recorded inscriptions; or indeed they may well hold transcripts themselves, as does the Society of Australian Genealogists for much of New South Wales.

Shee first deceased. Hee for a little Try'd

To live without her, liked it not & Dyd.

This is from a plaque in St Bartholomew's, probably London's oldest church. If it referred to ancestors of mine, I think it would be reasonable to assume that the couple's relationship had been a fond one?

Cemetery inscriptions can be particularly valuable where a date of death is unknown or the accepted date has failed to flush out a death certificate.

Newspapers and local business records can sometimes reveal a date of death where civil records have failed to do so.

Local Government

A phone call will bring you the where-to-go-for-information; and once you get there, something about what-there-is and how-to-get-at-it. Probably you'll be put in touch with a Public Relations Officer or an Archivist or a Local History Officer.

A good place to start might be the records of ratepayers. These are held under varying titles, as Assessment Book or Valuation Book. Check out what material there is for, say, grandmother's 1910 address or Aunt Flora's corner shop.

Then perhaps look through the ratepayers' rolls.

Do make sure you enlist whatever help the Local Authority offers, as there can be information hidden away that you'd never know to ask for. Here are examples of several kinds of documents you might expect to turn up:

- Ratepayer petitions
- Minutes of meetings
- Correspondence, general
- Lighting committee reports
- Return of buildings
- Improvements register
- Rate assessment books.

Also — the council, through its library, will almost certainly be able to direct you to any local history groups, or indeed to any local histories that have already been compiled or published.

These are unlikely to have specific information about your ancestors (though they just might, if those ancestors were wealthy or infamous enough!) but will have quite a deal about the world in which these ancestors laughed their joy and cried their grief.

Schools

Records at individual schools often go way back — in part, I expect, because public servants have learned that it's easier to explain why a record hasn't been destroyed than why it has!

These include academic records and the like (e.g. aptitude tests), which are probably confidential but which, so hoary now with time, many principals will make available; reports and programmes of school concerts; school magazines; examination and test results; year books and calendars; even a punishment book.

State education authorities have records too, though of course these vary from one to another. You could expect such authorities to have an Information Officer or equivalent; and that would be the place to start, with a phone call or letter. I have found few well-marked expressways in this area. One seeks out a track of one's own, enquiring as one goes.

Local newspapers will sometimes have printed items about district schools too — sports coverage, speech nights, student achievement and the like. You would in most instances approach such research with some specific dates.

Other institutions which might hold similar records are hospitals, societies (the Welsh Society — which destroyed most of their records just a few weeks before I came seeking them; and the Benevolent Society, which didn't!); records of meetings (the Bronte-Tamarama Progress Association, the Knott's Creek Labor Party Branch), employer records, solicitors' records, a register of stationers; local RSL or Leagues Clubs.

Our ancestors will have left footprints of the kind the above incomplete inventory can only suggest. It is up to the resourceful researcher to speculate where, in each particular case, these prints might be found.

Court Records

Some autobiographers might consider themselves fortunate *not* to find, this time, any such records for their family!

Court records are of all kinds (e.g., ecclesiastical) and in all locations (e.g. UK, Australia). Begin with enquiries at the appropriate archives repository.

Family lore claims that my grandfather once punched a priest on Epping Railway Station. This grandparent, a cheerful Irish Catholic, had married a Welsh Protestant (in an Anglican church!); and this, according (allegedly) to the priest, rendered the children illegitimate.

The assault charge is reputed to have been heard at Ryde Magistrates' court. I acknowledge and confess that I have never actually checked it out!

Here is an example of a press report of a court proceeding - from the (Sydney) Gazette of 1 June 1806:

> **A Bench of Magistrates assembled on Wednesday, before whom were examined Paul Randall, of Hawkesbury, settler, and Michael Brannan, his servant, on suspicion of having been employed or concerned in the distillation of spirituous liquors, contrary to, and in defiance of, the General Orders forbidding that noxious practice under certain penalties prescribed.**
>
> **Upon the evidence of John Green, a constable, it appeared that part of a still had been by him detected in the possession of Brannan; whereupon a search was ordered by the resident Magistrate to be made about his master's premises, where several requisites to this illicit purpose being discovered, a warrant was issued to apprehend him.**
>
> **The Bench considering the offence to demand a closer investigation, and determined to make every necessary measure for the abolition of this practice, committed the servant, upon whom a part of the still was found, for further examination before a full Bench of Magistrates in Sydney; and permitted the master at large, provisionally upon his appearing when required.**

Directories

The Post Office Directory is likely to be the most useful. Even smaller libraries will often have copies going many decades back. Through these you can track down who lived where, when; and follow those who change addresses.

Here are three of the characters we are familiar with located by the Post Office Directory for NSW for 1871:

Seymour, Mrs HF, innkeeper, Windsor Street, Richmond.

Sly, WM senior, groom, Windsor Street, Richmond.

Sly, WM junior, butcher, Boswell Street, Richmond.

There are also Directories medical, legal, university, trade, even street. The skill is to track down those appropriate to your own searches.

Parish Maps

These record land purchases (or grants) of Crown Land, with county maps recording transactions involving larger areas. Such maps give names and sometimes dates of first purchasers which could turn out family. Parish/county maps are held by the Department of Lands and may be bought.

Newspapers

Huge quantities of information reside here, but likely not a great deal for the average autobiographer unless there has been some measure of celebrity in the life or the family. Information here can prove elusive too, unless you have strong leads to it or precise references.

It is possibly best to start general searches at a Reader Assistant Desk in a library with a substantial newspaper-holding — Australian dailies, or overseas, or religious, or trade — and best, too, to have your request as specific as possible.

As will be apparent from the above paragraph, one is not restricted to the major dailies. Indeed, a small-town bi-weekly or a monthly Public Works Digest could well hold more information on your subject(s).

Press clippings can also prove helpful if there is anyone in your sights sufficiently "well known" to draw public attention. Newspapers frequently have their own clippings libraries, but the extent to which outsiders are permitted to use these can be discovered only through enquiry.

Funeral Notices, Death Notices and Obituaries can be a rich source of matter, particularly as you are likely to have a date-of-death or near-abouts for tracking down. The first two will sometimes sort out some of the extended family relationships for you.

My Great Uncle Johnny, for instance — the eight year old brother in Frances Purcell's manuscript of her childhood on a Surry Hills dairy — existed in family legend as a brilliant young man destined for the ministry who went wrong somehow (there's some hint of "the drink") and abandoned wife and family. He ended up in squalor and yet did pioneer work for pensioners and allegedly had the biggest funeral the suburb of Newtown had ever hosted.

Some of this came together when, amongst estate papers, I came across an obituary:

LATE MR LEPHERD'S FUNERAL
Pensioners' Friend Is Buried
Fine Tributes

The remains of the late Mr Jonathan Lepherd, former president of the Old-Age and Invalid Pensioners' Association, were interred in the Church of England portion of Randwick Cemetery yesterday afternoon. Prior to the funeral a service was held in the Methodist Church, Newtown.

The Rev. Walker, who officiated at the church service, spoke of the kindness and generosity of the late Mr Lepherd and of how he had worked for the old-age and invalid pensioners. Their troubles, he said, were his troubles. He was one of the greatest workers for the restoration of the pension to $1 a week, and at last his labors were rewarded. He had lived just long enough to see the full pension restored.

There follows quite a list of moderately distinguished mourners and others present, and a photo captioned *"Old Soldiers in Life's War"* which shows Great Uncle Johnny as a cheerful-looking old rascal, tie and scruffy collar everywhere, hat tipped right back, not too much in the way of teeth.

Obituaries can also, unfortunately, be unreliable.

Read this of Sophia Sly, adopted daughter of Margaret Randal and Henry Francis Seymour:

> **One of the oldest and most respected, and also one of the best known residents of Richmond, in the person of Mrs Sophia Sly, of Marsh Street, passed away to that bourne from whence no traveller returns on Friday morning last, at the age of 75 years. The deceased was a native of Richmond. She had been ailing for a long time prior to her death. Many years ago she kept the Black Horse Hotel, now occupied by her son William, and one thing that characterized her long life was her liberality and kindeartedness. She leaves a large number of sons and daughters and a larger number of grand and great grand children.**

There follows an account of the funeral service, where both Rev. J. Howell Price and Rev. Dr Cameron made "frequent reference to the life of the deceased", and a description of the coffin, "of polished cedar, mounted with silver (and) covered with beautiful wreaths".

What the obituary of this respectable and handsomely despatched old lady hedged was that she was the daughter of two convicts — James Westbrook and Elizabeth Phipps — who had been adopted by Henry Francis Seymour, a convict and Margaret Randall, daughter of two convicts; and that she'd married a convict, William Sly! But, apart from those ... !

We might, of course, behave equally evasively in similar circumstances; but for the autobiographer, it's a caution: how much can be suppressed and distorted by respectability and its hundred gigs.

Most valuable are probably the *Sydney Gazette* and from 1832 onwards the *Government Gazette.* These report land sales and grants, civil appointments, police records and — almost — you name it! And the holdings have been indexed — as the following for Paul Randall, *Sydney Gazette*, 1803-1826:

Charged with illicit distillation, June 1, 1806.

Part of farm for sale by execution, Oct. 1, 1809. Signatory to Hawkesbury Settlers Address, Dec. 8, 1810. Govt. cattle issues to, June 22, 1816. Notice re lost store receipt, Feb. 20, 1819. Hotel licence issued to, Richmond, Feb. 24, 1820. Spirit licence, Richmond, Feb. 24, 1821. Hotel licence, March 22, 1822.

Musters and Censuses

These relate to early Australia and are basically lists of residents.

Copies of each have been widely distributed of late years so lots of libraries now have these records available. Presumably you'd be approaching with a name or names to check out.

The type and amount of information varies from one muster/census to the next, but can prove very useful.

For example, from the 1828 census:

SLY, William. TL Guildford 1812 Life Landholder Windsor 38 Pro. Overseer to Arch. Bell.

Thus — William Sly, a Ticket of Leave convict, was transported on the *Guildford* for Life and is now a landholder at Windsor, aged 38, Protestant, overseer for Archibald Bell. This is from the 1806 Muster:

Paul Randall. Grant Richmond Hill 30 acres.

Wheat 10 ac, maize 6 ac, barley 1{1/2} ac, potatoes 1 ac, pasture 12 ac. Hogs 32, 2f In hand: maize 10 bush. Proprietor, wife and one child not victualled.

The "not victualled" simply means that the family were self-supporting and not requiring government assistance with food rations. Because of the doubtful literacy of many conducting the muster/census, and the ease with which transcription errors occurred (from handwriting, both here and in the United Kingdom), they can prove unreliable.

Churches

These have been much covered in other sections.

Mainly, they contain registers of baptism, marriage and burials, but there could also be confirmation and other such records. Parish magazines can also hold information, if you've some idea where to look for it. And of course there exist memorial plaques and the like both within the church building and on outside walls.

As stated earlier, a good deal of such material will already have been transferred to some more central and public storage system, as State Archives.

The Australian Society of Genealogists publishes booklets detailing its holdings of church records.

The initial approach for specific church records could be through the local clergyman or priest; or alternatively, through a capital city Head Office for direct enquiry concerning the whereabouts of particular records (for example, the History Commission of the Roman Catholic Diocese of Melbourne, or the Australian Jewish Society).

Convict Records

That is, records specific to convicts. There are many general sources, as court records and registers of births, deaths and marriages, which hold information about individuals who happen *also* to be convicts.

Convict records are actually not as helpful to many autobiographers as one might assume, because the greater number of Australians happen *not* to be descended from convict stock.

Since World War II, particularly, a considerable proportion of the population finds its origins in continental Europe, Asia, the Middle East, the Americas, the Pacific and even Africa.

In any case, the greater number of those sourced from the United Kingdom were free immigrants, particularly after the

1830s and accelerating mid-century with the gold rushes and immigration waves generally.

Over the whole convict period, only some 160,000 left their country for their country's good. A considerable proportion even of these, particularly early on, had relatively restricted opportunity to breed, being at times incarcerated, and with females proportionately few.

If you do want to trace back to Jenny Blake in a line up at the Parramatta Female Factory, start with State Archives and State Libraries.

First, and most importantly, request any leaflets or brochures that will guide you. These will be more use than any general instructions from a text like this, because they will be directed at the particular institution's own holdings and procedures.

Broadly, though, the first record of a particular convict would usually be from an Assize or Quarter Session record in the UK.

You would probably most readily get to this through the Ship's Indent for the particular convict you are searching — that is, the list of convicts on a particular vessel and information both personal and official on each. The latter should include a *tried where/when* section, as:

Southampton Assizes, 27 Feb. 1836 L(ife) Middlesex Gaol delivery, 16 Sept. 1812.

If, as is often the case, there are in Australia no copies of the court records you want, you must send away for them to the appropriate County Record Office or whatever in the United Kingdom.

For information about such applications, go to volumes which guide ancestry searches in greater detail.

I have, however, always found the following letter paradigm quite satisfactory:

The Records Officer,
Lancashire County Record Office,
Sessions House,
Lancaster Road,
Preston, Lancs.

Dear Records Officer,

I would be very grateful if you could let me have a photo copy of the trial transcripts, together with any associated material, for Henry Francis Seymour, Lancaster Assizes, March, 23, 1816.

Please let me know whatever fees are involved in this and I will forward cheque for same. Thank you for whatever assistance you can give me in this.

Yours sincerely,

An enquiry to Middlesex brought forth this conspiratorial gem from 22 year old James Westbrook, father of Sophia Sly. The letter was presented as evidence in Westbrook's trial for theft in 1812. (Sophia's mother, Elizabeth Phipps, was charged with the same crime. Each was found guilty; and a death sentence commuted to transportation. James' brother Samuel seems to have dodged the net!)

Dear Brother,

This comes, with my kind love to you, hoping to find my sister and you in good health as it leaves me. I shall take it a great favour, if you will let me know how things are settled, for I have heard that James Wyman has been with him, and is letting him have the things back again. I will meet you at the Bricklayers Arms. Do not fail coming.

James Westbrook.

The addresses for County Record Offices can be obtained from Genealogical Societies and recent family history publications.

The name of the ship on which your ancestor was transported will be noted in a number of convict records, as tickets-of-leave and pardons, some census and musters, even sometimes on a burial certificate under "If Bond, Name of Ship".

For a more detailed and extensive guidance for using convict records in searches as above, see the excellent *Guide To Convict Records* in the Archives Office of New South Wales.

Mostly the trial records you will turn up in the United Kingdom will be brief, just a few lines detailing the offence (frequently with a list and valuation of stolen items) and penalty.

The Old Bailey transcripts, on the other hand — taken down by a court reporter — are quite extensive and wondrously revealing of character and of the times.

Here is one that explains how Mary Randall managed to end up in New South Wales when, in 1792, her brother-in-law William Randall and his companion were charged with:

> **... burglariously and feloniously breaking and entering the dwelling houses of Thomas Gibbons, about the hour of ten in the night, of 8th of April last, and burglariously stealing therein a silver watch, value 30s. one pair of shoes, value 2s. two silver table spoons, value I6s. nine cotton gowns, value 9s. two gold wire ear-rings, value 2s. a pair of shoe and knee buckles, value 5s. and three guineas in monies, numbered, the property of Thomas Gibbons; seven gowns, value 3Is. three black cloaks, value 21s. one red ditto, value 10s. nine silk handkerchiefs, value 18s. two tuckers, value 2s. one half guinea, and a Spanish dollar, value 4s 6d. and property of Elizabeth Gibbons.**

There is also a list of property stolen (equally burglariously, no doubt!) from one Jane Mole, which includes a bank note of £10.

This was quite a rumbustious robbery. Thomas Gibbons, the victim, told how the intruders:

> **...threw something over my head; I was afraid to look up or open my eyes, as they swore they would blow my brains out.**

And Catherine Gibbons, the sister, confirmed this ruffian behaviour.

> **... two men came into the bar, one with a pistol, the other with a cutlas: the man with the cutlas desired of me to lie down, or he would cut my head off: I laid down and he tied my head with a child's frock.**

Jane Mole, Gibbons' mother-in-law, added that:

... after they had taken what they pleased, they supped upon cold roast pork, and sucked 15 eggs.

Mary Randall entered the scene charged with "feloniously receiving part and parcel of the said goods, knowing them to have been stolen". Here — the evidence of Elizabeth Payne — is what did for her:

I lived in Mary Randall's house. She kept an oil shop. She lived in the ground floor under my room. I was at home on the night of Easter Sunday, to the best of my knowledge, about nine o'clock. I was coming down stairs with a lighted candle, then I saw five men go into Mary Randall's apartments; William Randall had a blue jacket on; I was out about a quarter of an hour that night; I returned and Mrs Randall's door was shut; I went to bed, and about three on Easter Monday morning I was awakened by some men talking; I sat upright in my bed, and the first word I heard one of them say, that they had had a better supper that night than for some time; I knew William Randall's voice above the rest; he said he had his skin full of liquor; I heard one of them say they had had fine fun with the boy, and Mrs Randall made answer it was a pity they had not cut off all their heads; then one of the men seemed to be very sick in the yard; I opened my shutter and window softly and saw it was Leman Baker; I saw his face very plain; there was a candle burning, but it was dawn of day then, or moonlight; they came into the back room and some of them said what have you done with the black cloaks; then somebody said they had not them and they began to wrangle; then somebody said you have planted them (which I understood hid) and somebody said let us count the gowns, and they counted one and twenty; my apartment is over the back room and when they went into the fore room I could not hear what they said ...

... On Tuesday Polly Randall the little girl brought me a scarlet cloak, bound with scarlet ribbons, and told me her mother desired me to pawn it, and some silk handkerchiefs, which I refused; the girl left the cloak hanging at the back of my chair; she came and told me she had told her mother; and took the cloak and pawned it.

... Early the next morning the girl came up and desired me to pawn a gown; I said I was sure that was too big for her mother and asked where she got it. Upon this question the girl seemed to be surprised and said they were theirs ... and told me she was afraid that her mother's apartment might again be searched.

Elizabeth Payne's evidence was substantially corroborated by John Cook, head borough, who searched Mary Randall's house and found pawn tickets and stolen goods; and pawnbroker Gardner himself, who declared:

Mary Randall pledged these six pieces of cotton (produces the cotton) with me and said they were for her mother.

Mary Randall proceeded to her "defence":

I am a widow. This woman came to me on Easter Wednesday and brought a cloak, and begged that I would go and pawn it; I said no, but the child might go; which she did, and brought me 10s. she gave me the duplicate; she said she knew of a good speak, and she would row in it; my Lord, she knows I am a lone woman, and that this girl was the eldest of seven children that I had to work for; she said she had plenty of plants, and she knows there were a cutlas and an iron crow found up her chimney. I hope your Lordship will consider my case.

His Lordship, Mr Justice Ashbury, no doubt did consider her case — but not favourably!

Mary, wife of Paul Randall, GUILTY. Transported for fourteen years.

Such transcripts, if they exist for any of your ancestors, can recreate the persons and their world to a thrilling extent.

Amongst other convict records you will be directed to by particular guides to particular archives and the like are: ticket-of-leave papers, which include magistrates' "butt books"; pardons; UK journals for accounts of original trials and local journals for any subsequent misdemeanours publicised; court bench books, government correspondence.

Here is an example of the latter — to D. Wentworth, Principal Surgeon, from Governor Macquarie, dated 1 April 1817.

Dear Sir,

The Bearer Henry Seymour having been a Surgeon and a Person of this description being much wanted at Bathurst, I have resolved on sending him thither — to be permanently stationed there till further orders as an Acting Assist Surgeon. I therefore request you will be so good as to furnish him with a small assortment of medicines this evening packed up in a small box to take with him thither; as, he is to set out tomorrow morning, in case the weather is good, along with Mr Evans for Bathurst.

Yours truly, L. Macquarie.

Military

If you've a forebear who was in the military and you know either the name or number of the regiment, you'll likely have available quite an amount of record. There is somewhat less for marines.

Begin perhaps with *The Historical Records Of New South Wales* and/or whatever else your archives or library suggest and offer. Such documents as the Quarterly Pay Lists and the several monthly military returns should eventually lead you to a date of arrival in Australia and a ship.

For later information about serving personnel, apply to the Australian War Memorial, Canberra.

Books

This term is intended to cover other people's (auto)biographies, correspondence (published, as against letters-in-a-drawer), diaries and journals, reminiscences, *belle lettres*, dictionaries of biography — any volumes which contain some reference, particularly of a personal nature, to "your people" and their times.

Even if you come across no pages detailing anything specific about your *personae*, you might well find an account of the street or suburb your great-great lived in, or an organisation she/he belonged to and attended; or a soap-making process you'd heard about from Gran but never really understood; or a description of a Royal visit Great Aunt Delia had attended but noted with only minimal detail in her journal.

It is self-evident that any of the above would allow you to fill out your own account; to furnish that remote world more evocatively with sights, sounds, colours, movement, emotions.

The final suggested source to draw on for family tree differs from those to date in both nature and reliability. It is discovered in the next section, *Memories*.

Memories

It might seem at first consideration that these can go back only that certain distance — namely, within the minds of those still living.

Mostly, this is so. But there is also that small category of memories within memories — memories *of* memories. Which, if your more fortunate stars are in the ascendant, can turn up items that, because of the nature of what gets itself remembered in the first place and then passed on in the memory of another, are quite important and likely to prove fascinating.

My Great Grandmother Ann Jones came out from Wales in 1856, in the vessel before the ill-fated *Dunbar*, which in a storm mistook Sydney Heads and drove into cliffs, with all-but-one aboard perishing.

Ann was young, and alone. She'd left a stable family with a seemingly prosperous greengrocery business in Llandysul, Cardiganshire, for a raw colony where she knew not a soul, and done so without any particular skills whatsoever.

Now why on earth ...?

There were two passed-on "memories" about this.

The first was that she had what was then termed "a weak chest". This seemed precious little to offer as explanation for so mighty and fateful a venture.

And yet — her daughter, Frances Lepherd/Purcell, living at Coogee, around the turn of the century, had seven children die within a year of birth, of "bronchitis". The doctor's judgement was that she would successfully rear infants only if she moved to a drier area. So she did this, shifting westwards, to Epping. Six of the seven progeny after that lived into their eighties; with the seventh still managing mid-sixties before departing (in an asthma episode!).

Indeed, this family "weak chest" continues to plague right into the present generation, bronchitics and asthmatics popping up even amongst 1990 littlies.

So the "memory" actually becomes not just plausible, but even adequate, if Ann's "chest weakness" had promised to prove terminal unless she emigrated?

It's also a moving explanation, if one reflects upon its human implications.

You will be aware by now of what would be the next step with all these certificates and extracts and transcriptions and testamentary documents. Writing them up; transforming them into autobiography.

The principles and procedures involved in this have been dealt with in earlier sections of this volume.

It is worth reminding, though, that the possibilities in doing this range from simply reproducing your documents, with little or no comment, in chronological order, to a fully dramatised narrative.

The example below is towards the latter pole. You will be able to tell from the quotation marks what is the documentary material being exploited here.

On 13th April, 1790, a labourer was sentenced at the Reigate Court, Surrey, "for a felony". He was "to be publickly Whipt at the Carts tail on Monday 19th Instant between the hours of 12 and 2 until his back is bloody from the White Lyon at Streatham to the space of Two hundred yards".

He was also "ordered to be transported for the Term of Seven Years to such parts beyond the Seas as His Majesty in his Privy Council shall be pleased to appoint and direct".

This is somewhat confusing as the same man, this time a "dealer in rope", on 13th July that same 1790, and still at Reigate, pleaded guilty to receiving "25 pounds Weight of Rope knowing the same to have been stolen" and was fined

One shilling; whereupon he "paid the Sheriff in Court and (was) discharged".

What is clearer, however, is that when Paul Randall, of Rotherhithe and St Johns, left his brother William, his wife Mary and a number of children, and set out in the convict ship "Admiral Barrington" for New South Wales, the human history of Richmond's Black Horse Hotel might be said to have had its genesis. [AUTHOR'S EXAMPLE]

Here is another and more sophisticated example of writing up from material. As you read it, work out the kinds of source which might provide each item of information. Ponder, too, the ways each of the items has been woven into a "story".

It seems most likely that the child Sophia Westbrook came to the Inn as a "help", perhaps with just board and lodging, as one would not be at all surprised to find the Westbrook children somewhat neglected. To stay on for the rest of her life, as she did, she must certainly have engaged the hearts of the childless Seymours as well as proved a competent employee or partner; and certainly on the death of Margaret Seymour the Inn became hers, along with several other blocks, cottages and farms. The story that has come down is that the Inn was left her in recognition of her caring for Margaret Seymour during her last illness. The will puts it thus: "in consideration of her long and faithful services and her unremitting kindness to me during a period of forty years ... " From being something fairly close to a penniless waif of convicts, Sophia had come within a few decades to modest wealth and respectability. She was to consolidate both.

Before she had finished with convicts, however, Sophia was to marry one. William Sly, a native of Surrey, was tried at Southampton in February 1836 for stealing the preceding December a gelding, said to be the property of a Mr Hackman of Lys. He was sentenced to life, and arrived at Sydney per the MOFFATT that same year. He was in his late teens — the records of his precise age are contradictory. He is simply noted, at the time of his conditional pardon in 1848, as a labourer; but it is likely that he had become a groom at the Inn some years before that. (Intriguingly, until the last couple of decades there were still Slys dealing with horses in the Richmond area — running Clydesdales!)

Anyway ... William must have been in the Hawkesbury district as he courted Sophia there; and on April 2, 1844, the couple were married by Rev. J.K. Walpole at St Peters. The consent for this was obtained from James Westbrook — for Sophia, aged only I7; and from the Governor for William.

Although Sophia's days at the Inn are much closer to our own than those of the Randalls and the Seymours, rather less is known about her. She and William produced 10 children, nine of which were living still in 1900; and the fact that these were named William, Mary, (Walter) Paul, Margaret, Sophia, Henry and Francis suggests that there was no disowning by her of parents and grandparents, but on the contrary, a strong sense of "family".

[AUTHOR'S EXAMPLE]

The "slim volume" of family history from which these two pieces are drawn exemplify some four types of source material — as follows:

- Formal documents
- Private sources like letters and diaries
- General works by others on the same people and/or periods
- What the author had himself experienced from the ancestors, directly or through the accounts of others.

For your own autobiography, you will need to decide whether you'll draw on all of the above or simply on the first two or three.

You will have to decide, too, when you write up documents and the like, to what extent and in what manner you will acknowledge these sources.

Masses of references add authority but also detract from readability and tend to diminish evocation of the person(s) and world(s) you are attempting to project.

Nil referencing, on the other hand, irritates anyone who might want to follow up some of your material further — someone from another family, for example. As well, it would reduce the history value of your production.

A happy compromise might be to include in your text only the major and obvious references, as:

So as Aunt Eliza records in her diary for Nov. 6 ...

Other references not tied to particular statements in your chapters can be listed at the end of the chapter or volume — or indeed at the foot of the page on which the material itself occurs, though some find this both cluttering and an impediment to reading on from page to page. Whatever, these methods would allow anyone who really wished to, to track down your source for this-that-and-the-other.

For example, if anyone wanted to check out the following:

Uncle Ben and Aunt Eliza were married at Ballarat on February 12, 1904 ...

they would find the appropriate source in full or in summary in say Appendix I, *Official Sources*.

There are two final sources of information and guidance:

The Church of Jesus Christ of Latter Day Saints — the Mormons — has an enormous repository of "pedigree sheets" in Salt Lake City, Utah, USA, and is reputed to be generous in allowing outsiders access to the material.

It can be particularly valuable, as part of the information obtainable is names-and-addresses of others working your territory. Also, the holdings for "difficult" areas, like Eastern Europe, are reported as relatively strong.

One can access the Salt Lake City collection from a number of outside points, so a first step would be to contact local Mormons for assistance.

The other source is an obvious one — the many genealogical groups.

Again, contact directly to see what offers. Local phone contacts are listed opposite.

NSW	The Society of Australian Genealogists,	**(02) 247 3953**
ACT	Heraldry and Genealogical Society of Canberra Inc.	**(06) 295 1411**
NT	Genealogical Society of the Northern Territory Inc.	**(089) 817 363**
Qld	Genealogical Society of Queensland Inc.	**(07) 891 5085**
SA	South Australian Genealogical and Heraldry Society Inc.	**(08) 272 4222**
Tas.	Genealogical Society of Tasmania Inc.	**(003) 445 258**
Vic.	The Genealogical Society of Victoria	**(03) 663 7033**
WA	The Western Australian Genealogical Society Inc.	**(09) 271 4311**

To sum up:

No how-to text can guide you from go to whoa in family history searches, because the primary sources of information are so numerous and in a way so random and scattered, and they vary so greatly in nature and location. Also, the repositories of these sources differ in what they hold and sometimes in how they organise and give access to it.

This relatively brief account of the researching has presented mainly the kinds of material you are likely to find and suggested procedures to enable you most effectively, and with the least discouragement, to find it.

Here is just a representative scatter of the multiplicity of documents you will come across in archives/libraries:

- Magistrates Population Books, 1820-1825. Windsor, etc.
- Index to letters received by Colonial Secretary, 1821-1826
- Index to miscellaneous pardons, 1827-1874
- Index to School Records

- Colonial Secretary: Naturalisation and Denization Records, 1834-1904
- Applications to marry by special licences, 1819-1836
- Convict applications to marry, 1825-1851
- Colonial Secretary. Returns of applications for publication of banns, 1828-1841
- Annual return of convicts who died, 1867-1891
- Sydney City Coroner — Register of Inquests and Enquiries 1862-1926
- Register of unemployed, 1860
- Index to Quarter Sessions Criminal Cases, Sydney and Country, 1839-1847; 1850-1901
- Macquarie Street Asylum, Parramatta: Register of Admissions and Discharges 18/7/96 — 16/5/03
- Superintendent's Report Book, 6/1891 — 3/1893 Letters from patients, c1890-1919
- Bench of Magistrates: Proceedings 1788-1812
- County of Cumberland Bench Book 1788-1821
- Butts of Tickets of Leave, 1827-1875
- Medical Journals on convict ships
- Criminal Registers, Newgate 1791-1849.

And if you were heading after "Bankruptcies", say, at the NSW Archives, then you'd turn up, just for starters probably:

- Insolvency Index, 1842-1887
- Bankruptcy Index, 1888-1929
- Insolvency Files, 1842-1887
- Bankruptcy Files, 1888-1929

So — to return from this swarm of particulars to overview, your general approach should be:

- Get whatever basic information you can from certificates of birth, death and marriage, supplemented by other records like a Family Bible and reliable word-of-mouth.

- Front up at the major repositories of genealogical information and get sorted out on what is there and how you get at it. The three major such repositories are likely to be Government Archives, State Libraries and genealogical societies, particularly the Society of Australian Genealogists.
- Pursue those more peripheral sources that might or might not be outside the major repositories, as — local government and Lands Office.
- Incorporate more intimate records, like letters, diaries, personal possessions, recollections, oral history. There will be frustrating gaps and maddening delays, and some longeurs during the searches too; but overall you can expect to turn up a body of material that will prove of the greatest satisfaction to you and be *all my own work*!
- It does, though, take time, and patience, and some measure of resourcefulness.

Then you have only to write it up!

Chapter Seven

Autobiography as (Self)-Healing

"... that kindly blank-faced old confidante ... "

Centuries of experience demonstrate that we errant and so-vulnerable human wayfarers can often "write out" something of our most defeating of travails and frustrations and dilemmas, our most deeply embedded disablements and despairs.

John Donne, arguably the finest of seventeenth century English poets, certainly believed that such "utterance", such teasing-it-out in verse, could be restorative in this way.

I thought, if I could drawe my paines
Through Rimes vexation, I should them allay.

In our own century, Virginia Woolf's experience tends to confirm this. Her parents, Leslie and Julia Stephen, became for her a block to independent identity and destiny; which was sad really, because neither was any monster.

Leslie Stephen was a free-thinking editor, essayist and literary critic. He certainly made excessive demands on his daughters in his later years; but he also allowed Virginia free run of his extensive library, an unusual liberty in those days. Julia Stephen, for her part, was a woman beautiful and widely admired — "a caring presence", she was once termed. But also, allegedly, as the "Angel in the House", somewhat complicit in the great Victorian patriarchy.

Here is the novelist's own statement of the situation as she saw it, and of the liberating effect for her of writing them into her novel *To The Lighthouse*.

> **Until I was in my forties ... the presence of my mother obsessed me. I could hear her voice, see her, imagine what she would do or say as I went about my day's doing.**
>
> **"My dear, you are a young woman ... Be sympathetic; be tender; flatter; deceive; use all the arts and wiles of our sex. Never let anybody guess that you have a mind of your own.."**
>
> **Father's birthday. He would have been ... 96, yes, today; & could have been 96, like other people one has known; but mercifully was not. His life would have entirely ended mine. What would have happened? No writing; no books — inconceivable. I used to think of him and mother daily; but writing THE LIGHTHOUSE, laid them in my mind. And now he comes back sometimes, but differently. (I believe this to be true — that I was obsessed by them both, unhealthily; & and writing of them was a necessary act.)**

Simply placing them out there on the page put them at a safe distance, perhaps? Or, writing about them enabled her to see them as other people, objectively, for the first time? Was there even a reversal of the parent-child roles, the writing making her in a way the parent; and the parents, in turn, her offspring, out of her creative imagination?

Whatever, it seems that Woolf was most stable when, through writing, she was re-engaging her old familiar world, and that her episodes of breakdown tended to occur when she was without this form of self-writing, (self-righting?).

First, though, some general frame, before I deal specifically with autobiography as self-healing.

It has been stated, and wisely so, that works of literature address two basic questions: Who am I? Where is here?

That is, the exploration of two central relationships, everyone's two central relationships — with our own selves, and with our universe.

Autobiography as a mode, even if operating at a relatively unsophisticated level, is perhaps the kind of writing that most directly addresses those two questions and those two relationships.

Through the recording and interpreting of one's whole life — even some recomposition of this life — autobiography can effectively suggest *who* you are and *where* you are; and by extension, *what* and *where* you have been, and *what* you might become and *where* you might be heading.

Occupying an area somewhere in this territory is the exercise of autobiography-as-self-discovery and self-healing.

That's the general framing of the topic. Exploration of self, and of that self's world. Now back at ground level: how might it actually work, this writing about one's self and one's experiences? How do ghosts get exorcised, frogs turned into princes and old hags into beautiful maids? How are tempests stilled and torments eased, paths struck through dark forests?

The most obvious answers would be those suggested in the references above to John Donne and Virginia Woolf — that by "writing out" what is oppressing us and is deflecting us from the fulfilled life, we somehow transpose the demons from "in here" to "out there". We relocate a great psychic weight some place else.

John Donne claimed that grief could be "tamed" through the discipline of writing poetry ("numbers").

Griefe brought to numbers cannot be so fierce,

For, he tames it, that fetters it in verse.

If this dark and wounding entity that is our grief — or rage, or fear, or shame, or whatever — can be thus exteriorised, it is also rendered open to scrutiny. You can size it up realistically because you see it from outside, then ponder strategies for dealing with it.

Indeed, the very act of writing — perhaps even simply of deciding to write — is already "dealing with it" to an extent, as an assertion of some authority over it, over your life. Thus occurs a reversal of relationship and role between self and whatever-is-the-shadow, the beast — a reversal subtle but significant, and empowering.

Next ...

Reason and intellect seem not greatly in fashion these past several decades: it's instinct, intuition, body knowledge and the subjective that the cognoscenti more favour. My own experience, which I needs must follow, is that nothing beats the Torch of Reason for a first approach to any problem. So that it's head, rather than heart, that I'd bring initially to whatever I'd written or had in mind to write.

Eventual resolution, of course, might well lie in the realm of emotion and spirit — with an Earth God rather than with Sky God; but it could be Head God, not Belly God, that guides one through those first searchings. If Fortune favours, your explorations into self might well uncover only some mini-problem that happens to be throwing a disproportionately large shadow. An antagonist less daunting and more tractable than you'd feared.

This is something of what happened to me when, in late teens, I went through what in those days was termed a "crisis of faith".

One anguished response was to write to a friend explaining, in the dreariest detail I've no doubt, my difficulties with such trusty doctrines as the divine inspiration of the Scriptures, and with the whole notion of a benevolent deity running our botched universe.

Setting all this out as ordered statement certainly dealt with my problem — by demolishing it!

Those troubling theologies, spread out over pages like a landscape beneath an aircraft, were rendered (to me) so transparently the product of human fears, of human flight from unwelcome realities, of an impulse to propitiate, and of the sad human capacity for self-deception that I abandoned them forthwith.

Putting all this to paper gave an overview ... and release. Not all readers will share my conclusions here, of course; but speak as find? Certainly I have since lived, and richly too, by the secular ideals and values of that many-petalled flower, civilisation.

Thus it is that writing-it-out might be seen to work; externalising problems and morbidities; putting them at paper-distance. And determining whether you need to gird up against some real monster, or simply against a ferocious looking paper tiger. Then planning your responses accordingly.

Reconstruction

Quite an amount has been written about this practice. Much of this lies within the expertise of the professional psychotherapist and beyond my responsible competence. But as I understand it, reconstruction goes something like this.

First, you locate the area(s)-in-time where occurred those episodes or situations which you see as having distorted or truncated something of your life and/or your identity.

This frequently seems to have been in childhood; and less frequently (but much too often) to "little girls". The blighting experiences themselves can range from simple neglect, through periods with parents/guardians/teachers repressive or even hostile, to outright violence and even sexual abuse.

Next, through a manner of meditation, a sort of journey of the imagination into your past, you return to those early periods and attempt to reinhabit them, seeking more constructive outcomes this time around.

Gloria Steinem, in her *Revolution From Within*, surveys the theories and procedures of reconstruction.

Through guided meditation she recalls herself as a child and dwells on this image, this mental photograph, then expands it to include particular surroundings of that Past — a yard, a garden, a puppy or kitten, a father or grandparent.

This way, it is believed, whole segments of that child-past can be projected and experienced.

Her own words, about herself:

It was odd to discover this untamed and spontaneous child: someone who existed before the terrifying years of living

alone with my mother, and who was shut out when I built a wall to protect me from what happened a few years later. She is so much more physical, confident, true to herself than I am. ... My ability to shut out feelings ... had closed a door on a part of myself.

The author sees such explorations as, amongst other things, a means of "retrieving and healing past traumas".

Effectively, if not literally, one relives those years from childhood to now, reprocessing something of the destructive or depriving experiences.

Where autobiography enters all this, it would seem, is as an instrument to make the process both more extensive and deeper — and probably more ordered — and hence more permanent in outcome.

That is, you write it all down — the scenes and episodes and the inner landscapes you associate with this child-that-was (and reflections on these too) — as they arise.

Such a re-childing, as it is sometimes termed, doesn't customarily generate chapters of formal and ordered prose. While at a later date you might well want to organise and shape these revisiting experiences, using writing skills as effectively as you can, initially you are setting out to produce material at random.

And these notes themselves?

They can range from straightforward descriptions of settings to extended narrative episodes. They can include the most fragmentary accounts of feelings recalled; of images and emotions and words and phrases of that childhood world; even records of waking fantasies and of dreams that seem associated in any way. (So keep a notebook handy by the bed!)

Autobiography-as-healing must by definition be more than just curiosity-driven-writing to discover items about yourself and your life generally. There should additionally be an intention to enlarge and define this newly revealed individual into a personality more free to choose and more effective in pursuing what has been chosen.

Beyond this again — you could be looking to exorcise some particular haunting that operates destructively throughout your Today life. Because as the nineteenth century poet Emily Dickinson pointed out:

One need not be a chamber to be haunted.

One need not be a house.

THE BRAIN has corridors ...

If something like this is your mission, it would almost certainly be an advantage and safeguard to enlist a skilled professional in whom you have confidence and with whom you are at ease.

Diary-writing

Apart from engaging such qualified assistance, the most one-to-one mode for such therapy is probably the diary; and of course it is no great leap from that to autobiography. One transliterates readily into the other.

Would-be diarists use all manner of means to put all manner of material on record.

Nor does it have to be the daily stint at the desk. The salesperson in her car and the sharing male partner washing the vegies can dictate to recorders. Others might enter into journals first-up at sparrow-stir or with night-cap in hand.

Some concentrate on noting down hopes, ideals, prayers, loves, hates, satisfactions. Others detail responsibilities, difficulties, impending decisions.

Scrutiny can be brought to bear on family, work/career, personal relationships, the erotic life, time past.

It can be any entry whatsoever from the encyclopaedia of your life! Indeed, beyond even these — pencil sketches can be made, scenes painted, favourite hymns or croons or country music or folk dance melodies or death metal gathered; quotations noted, printed clippings collaged, your favourite writings of others copied out.

As a youth I filled a large exercise book with writings I particularly loved — mostly poetry — and heavily representative of Rupert Brooke and Robert Browning. (No, I've no theories about those R.B. But note that Robbie Burns *didn't* make it!)

Coming across this tatty volume recently, the first time for some decades, quite intensely (re)illuminated my inner world of those distant years. What intrigued additionally, and touched too, was to receive from a cousin at much the same time another exercise book, tea-coloured with age this one, of my grandmother's from the year before her marriage. There, well over a century ago, the same copying down of loved verse!

So — and this is central — the informing idea is that one writes freely and uninhibitedly into this diary, with the assumption, at this point anyway, that no one else will ever be reading the lines.

This should act to bring you to a less protective and so less evasive sighting of your inner self — the real you — not the one you dress up and selectively censor as you revolve it slowly for presentation to the world.

Once you know what you are, and accept that this *is* in fact what you are, you are ready to embark on appropriate renovations, or to switch directions, to unpack and repack some inner baggage, even a re-paint!

Also, the impact of this kind of completely free-diarising seems to be to propel people along some current of release, which in turn becomes, or at least facilitates, self-healing.

You have, additionally, the option of subsequently converting your material, with whatever editing you choose for the nonce, into straight autobiography, along the lines dealt with in earlier chapters.

Anyway, whether you keep such a diary simply for embarking on a voyage of self-discovery, or as therapy for more troubling legacies, you will be dealing with chapters and rhythms of your life, past and present and prefiguring future.

You will be seeing certain things differently, not just in themselves but as they fit in with and take form and significance from everything else; from you and from the universe.

It is difficult to see all this happening without in its turn occasioning changes within you, and hence to your life of both today and tomorrow.

This somewhat revolutionary sort of diary — revolutionary because of its potential to challenge established inner paradigms and assumptions and certainties, even to overthrow and supplant deeply embedded personal visions — this somewhat revolutionary sort of diary need not and probably should not be any sort of "book of days" — that is, written to fit the calendar. This sort of thing:

Sunday 14th. To Camden Town for newspapers and milk. Phoned Susie re opera tickets. Letters to Ben and the Johnstones. Baltimore Road insurance. National Gallery, 2 x £2.40. Returned via Baker Street and Regents Park. Cold grey morning but pale sun pm, windless. 5 - 9. Inspired to neck chop stew again, with turnips.

[AUTHOR'S EXAMPLE]

This inventory of infinite boredom — well, perhaps some flicker from the lamb chops and turnips? — is from my records (I can scarcely dignify it with the term journal) of a London stint some years back. There are seven full months of the same! It's what one diarist called a "sausage and haddock" entry. My defence is that the document's purpose was entirely practical, much of it as a record for taxation purposes.

The kind of diary you'll be looking to produce, however, will follow some inner calendar of its own. It has its provenance in the confessional and self-monitoring journals of earlier centuries; though yours, I trust, will prove a good deal less narrow in outlook than these.

The Puritan diary, for example, for the most part dealt only incidentally with the public world. It concentrated rather on inner life, particularly with the diarist's preoccupation with his/her eternal soul; and concomitantly, with a great phantasmagoria of beckoning temptations and with searching for divine guidance and reassurance.

However, if one ignores the particular theologies and punitive assumptions that underlie these Puritan records, and regards more their generating principles and broad functions, then intriguing similarities to our own "therapy" diaries emerge.

For the Puritan man or woman, for example, the spelling out of a temptation might deflect that temptation, by making self-deception more difficult and also reinforcing resistance.

> **This afternoon I felt a strong desire to enjoy more liberty in thinking upon some vain thing which I had lately weaned myself from ... If I had not written this immediately ... I had almost been gone from this course and become plainly minded and idle as before.**

Also, journalising was such a widely approved activity that it enabled weakness and sin to be acknowledged without provoking too much condemnation from the community.

> **And do Thou instruct me how to write down my sins and Thy mercies, that I may not forget what Thou hast done for me, and what I have done against Thee.**

One might assume that much despair and guilt dissolved in the very act of externalising perceived sins onto non-judgemental paper.

The hazard with all this, of course, is that the recording of so much wickedness and failure might generate not healing but dismay — as seems to have occurred with seven year old John:

> **My John, on Lord's day sennight being Nov. 4, I being from home and my maid out of the house, at her return found him weeping bitterly, sore bleared, having begun it as he was reading a chapter. She of a long time could not get from him the cause; he still sobbed and took on very heavily. At last he told her it was because he had sinned against God and had offended Him ... Blessed be God for this beginning of God's work upon his heart.**

That's the Puritan journal, in many ways the ancestor of our diaries of today. One form of this latter has been described thus:

> **... a practical tool that enables you to express feelings without inhibition, recognise and alter self-defeating habits of mind ... come to know and accept the self which is you. It is a sanctuary where all disparate elements of a life can**

merge to give you a sense of wholeness and coherence. It can help you understand your past, discover joy in the present, and create your own future.

These lines are from Tristine Rainer's *The New Diary: How to Use a Journal for Self Guidance and Expanded Creativity.* It's a work of our own decade; yet substitute "sins" for "self-defeating habits" and "God" for "joy" ... ?

This *New Diary* I particularly commend, especially for those seeking the inward journey for its own experiences and rewards.

Ms Rainer, unlike many guidebook authors, actually knows a deal about the skills of writing. She is also sensible, and responsible towards her readers, eschewing the more extreme fashions and fads, and the jargon that goes with these.

Note, for example, her — "It can help ... " above. Some authors would have gone for — "It *will* help ... ", or even — "It will *enable* ... "; claims which cannot possibly be made with certainty and hence with integrity, because diary writing will not prove a wholly successful exercise for every single person who chooses to embrace it.

This author then lists several dozen benefits "most frequently mentioned" from the keeping of the *New Diary*; and again, note that cautious "most frequently mentioned". Not guaranteed!

Anyway, here are four of them, selected more or less at random just to convey the idea:

- A place to develop skills of self-expression
- A method for turning negative mental habits into positive energy
- A way to gain perspective on your emotions and resolve the past
- A means of keeping in touch with the continuity and rhythms of your own life.

There follows a brief history of journal writing.

American colonial women, for instance, kept diaries as record for later generations to read and to understand what they'd experienced and indeed endured. Nineteenth century Romantics on the other hand seem to have written more to assert and defend their ideas of the primacy of the individual, as against the authority of State or other such institution.

Ms Rainer outlines what she sees as the essential nature of *New Diary* writing. It will be:

> **.... free of ... conventions and rules. Everything and anything goes. You cannot do it wrong. There are no mistakes. At any time you can change your point of view, your style, your book, the pen you write with, the direction you write on the pages, the language in which you write, the subjects you include, or the audience you write to. You can misspell, write ungrammatically, enter incorrect dates, exaggerate, curse, pray, brag, write poetically, eloquently, angrily, lovingly. You can paste in photographs, newspaper clippings, cancelled cheques, letters, quotes, drawings, doodles, dried flowers, business cards, or labels. You can write on lined paper or blank paper, violet paper or yellow, expensive bond or newsprint.**
>
> **It's your book, yours alone. It can be neat or sloppy, big or little, carefully organized or as gravity-free as a Chagall landscape. Flow, spontaneity and intuition are the key words. You don't have to plan what you are going to do. You discover what you have done once you have set it down.**

These two paragraphs communicate the sometimes iconoclastic and almost libertarian spirit of this volume, and also its intelligence and energy. Further inventive devices for generating diary material follow.

For a start, to whom are you writing in your diary? That is, who are you addressing? Who do you have in mind as (eventual) reader?

Unless you've particular reason or impulse to the contrary, it's probably best in such immediate writing simply to be addressing yourself.

You might feel, though, that your diary is (also?) communicating with a counsellor. It would be a pity, and counterproductive, if this were to lead to any inhibition with your entries.

If on the other hand you are writing for an outsider — for a partner or grandchild or friend or whoever to read in due course

— then your focus will almost certainly be less immediate and probably less intimate. You will be having in mind more how all these entries might be looking some years along the way.

Such considerations influence both what you write and how you write it.

Virginia Woolf, incidentally, who is arguably the finest of all twentieth century diarists, wrote knowing that her husband Leonard would be reading her each day's entry. This isn't the intrusion it might sound, as she likewise read his diary entries; but one must wonder what the influence would have been on her emotional equilibrium had she been able to address herself in full and assured privacy?

Tristine Rainer certainly urges *New Diarists* to shun all faltering and inhibition. You put down whatever presents itself, and let judgement and sorting out follow later. However embarrassing or proscribed or unintelligible or plain boring stupid — in content or in expression!

No one else need ever see your pages — if that's what you'd prefer. It can all be erased.

Whereas anything you *don't* get down on paper, likely spins away forever into the evanescing past.

Anyway, those too-embarrassing fragments, or the deeply troubling ones; if you preserve them, they might prove of value later. As significances not noted at the time become apparent or they serve as springboards to elsewheres that *will* prove productive.

If you are writing at all for a therapist to share, then any contradictions should be allowed to stand — as, how you felt about Anna on Sunday and your reversed feelings by Thursday. The ambivalence could be significant and initiate discussion and exploration.

Whereas if you are writing for some further-in-the-future reader, and hence probably more deliberately and objectively, those incompatible feelings about Anna might profitably be "averaged" into a general attitude.

Write also, to the extent that it proves possible, when the inner voice speaks. It can prove a fickle communicator, not obliging with replay to order.

A further suggestion is that you give to your pages *opinions and feelings* as well as straightforward accounts of happenings.

It might be, for instance, that you scorn what you see as your sister's snobbery and hypocrisy; or that you feel strong attraction to a colleague of your own gender; or that you've embarked on an affair with your partner's best friend.

A "healing" approach could be seen to urge you to write all this out, without restraint, even if only as a temporary and private measure that later you'll completely erase.

With more straightforward autobiographing, however, considerations of taste, compassion or simply self-protection might lead you either to mute your account or indeed to keep silent altogether.

Finally, if you just can't get started with all this *New Diarising*, try writing up what you see as the most important event for you since you first embarked on this self-project.

Write up the event and its importance, writing it as it comes. Then rewriting it, if necessary, to the extent that you need to get it more exactly as it was, all in balance, the feelings too.

Here's a bare event:

The time my mother didn't know me when I got home, and later told me someone had called in looking for me!

[AUTHOR'S EXAMPLE]

This is what happened to a friend of mine — Richard — and would certainly for him have been a contender for any "most important ...". Here's how it was finally written up:

I was staying a fortnight with my rapidly aging mother, doing some business in the city; and when I walked in one night after work she stared at me and said —

"If you're looking for Richard, he's not home yet. He shouldn't be long."

I just bolted around to the local and downed two stiff Scotches. Then, still somewhat shaken, returned.

"There was some man here looking for you," my mother greeted me calmly. "He didn't say who he was."

I've rendered this more as an episode in an autobiography than as a diary entry — can't help it! — but you could write it as if you were telling someone in a letter. You might well want to expand on your feelings too. We must feel free to do such writings in our own way.

Then perhaps as a further freeing-up; the loveliest colour you've encountered recently; a house? a wall? an artefact? carpet? flower? item of clothing or simply a length of fabric? And not only the *what*, also the *how* loveliest.

If I were writing this, I think I'd do a paragraph about the flowers in our local cemetery, beside the blue Pacific. A few weeks back my granddaughter and I counted eighteen different varieties displaying their palette-strokes in the sunny nor' easter. Now, just a few weeks later, there are really only coreopsis making much show — dabs of Jersey butter, tossing over the Sleepers like Wordsworth's daffodils.

If folk knew, they'd come in coachloads!

Next, you could perhaps write up your most unsatisfactory business or shopping episode and how you responded to this. Or if there hasn't been one of either, then the most unsatisfactory personal encounter.

The nature of such an incident would determine its length. Don't flinch from trying to reconstruct any dialogue involved. You'll no doubt get your contribution to those testy exchanges much wittier second time round anyway!

Finally, try putting together the most moving link with the past that has crossed your path in recent months — or years, if you need to go back so far for an effective example.

Mine was to go overseas shortly after my father-in-law died. He had customarily — across decades! — demanded the most detailed accounts of such peregrinations, as:

"You didn't explain how you and the kids got all that baggage from Euston to Waterloo."
[AUTHOR'S EXAMPLE]

We were so very conscious, all the time we were away this venture, of what we *would* have been writing to him if ... "

Anyway, if freely and persistently you set about writing up all of these, or similar of your own choosing, you'll find yourself well on the way with your *New Diary*.

If that starter motor still won't crank over, you could try simulating a letter to a real friend or simply to an imaginary partner contracted for the purpose. Those of you who write letters frequently would likely find such a ploy momentum-generating. Then, when you get to the end of the pages, you need simply erase the "Dear and Valued Whoever" and the epistle becomes *New Diary*.

Emotions

Ms Rainer goes on to devote many pages to detailing and discussing techniques for exploiting one's self as resource, then replicating in diary form something of this procedure.

As her methods are both sensible and innovative, and as much that she writes is readily transposable to any form of autobiography, I'll wander around several of her suggested headings and kick-start points.

One can use these diary pages simply to register strong feelings — emotions. So write it all down. You love her, you despise her — as direct speech, if you like.

I've been betrayed — and by my closest friend.

It's been a brute of a day. Johnno left this morning, without one word of explanation. Celie hasn't phoned, though it's well over the hour. And the damn bloody bathroom's flooded...

I said, as patiently as I could —

"Mum, it's not that I think you're going to die soon. I hope you'll live another twenty years. But you should have a will. Everybody who has assets should have one. Particularly when we have these family ... situations. Dell in the clinic. The mortgage. It should all be provided for, because none of us know ... "

"You always did try to upset me ... "
[AUTHOR'S EXAMPLES]

There might be times when you'll want to move beyond such "dailiness" to more general and continuing strong feeling about things and issues.

What are you hostile towards? Not just momently, but as a steady state:

- *Political and religious fundamentalists*? You resent strongly the way these attempt, sometimes brutally, to force on you beliefs and behaviour that you see as quite without any reasonable basis and likely to prove very destructive?
- *Folk who are racist, sexist*? Or to switch poles — those who exploit anti-discrimination legislation for their own self-interested ends?
- *The thriftless* who, you maintain, fritter away their own money and then expect to live and be hospitalised, etc. out of your taxes? Or trade unions? Or corporate high-fliers? Or students? Or yuppies?

You could also write of *moments* of emotion, as well as about *objects*.

Your wonder at the birth of a child? My wife "helped" at the birth of a grandson, did the photography! It proved an enormously moving moment. Your equally marvelling at someone's tangible expression of love; from a child, a partner, a parent, a friend; even from a pet! Grief at loss through death, perhaps as you call by a memorial niche, or an anniversary occurs.

Desolation from ... pity from ... delight in ...

You could also, one might add, write about those feelings you seem *not* to have but would like to; and you could speculate about why you do not have them and what you might do about this.

For example, some individuals seem unable fully to love. They cannot identify wholeheartedly and unreservedly with another or with others, in a way that would make them automatically venture all in a loved one's happiness or defence or rescue.

Perhaps those unable fully and spontaneously so to love can get by on affection plus a strong sense of duty? Indeed, a few might feel that in practical terms, the latter pair do pretty much as well anyway!

There are in fact a number of other generally approved emotions, of varying degrees of importance, that many of us simply do not possess, or possess only in diminished measure.

An aesthetic sense, for example, that confident response to beauty and to art generally. It can be very undermining to have no real idea whether you should consider a painting or vase or piece of music ... "any good". Many students have come to fear, even to detest, poetry because they know they should be *feeling* something; but they don't.

One might well argue that too much attention is paid to what we *do* feel, to the neglect of what we *don't*, which could prove equally disabling.

"Feeling is first", declared the poet ee cummings, cautioning us all; and "who pays attention" only to "the syntax of things" will indeed "never wholly kiss"!

There is one caveat, however, with this writing about emotions. Might some best be left undisturbed?

Could they, at such an early and intense stage of self-exploration, perhaps carry fire and the sword to your inner self? After all, pariah feelings might wither away eventually of their own accord, in their own due season, or simply be swept away Pentacostally. Ever seen a desert inner-landscape flourish suddenly as a garden when a love affair enveloped; or even, if less dramatically, following a switch to a new career; or a child is born; or an addict really rehabilitated?

There's always, too, some possibility that a persistent problem can be insulated and so disregarded rather than cauterised. After all, it's what the oyster does — and gets a pearl out of it, they say!

Calm and objective consideration is called for with such decision-making, and perhaps some tapping of the wisdom of others. Not every problem is best dealt with by an artillery barrage followed by bayonet charge!

Somewhat overlapping *emotions* as a topic for diary entry is *description*, either as a resource or as a trigger for releasing inhibition, opening up the self. This can be word-painting of scenes, or the narration of events.

So, you could give a detailed description of the outlook from your verandah or study window or holiday cottage porch — word photos — or portraits of several friends, all together at a pub lunch, say; from what each is wearing to summaries of what each contributed to the conversation.

Or you could give an account of a "negotiating" session with a partner or child about allotted tasks or degrees of "space" in a relationship; even a review of a movie just seen, not simply a relating of the plot, though that could be the starting point. Also describe the film as a whole, its ideas and themes and techniques and mood; and outline too your response to it.

Reflection

A final technique is termed *Reflection*.

In its simplest form, this seems to run closest to just "writing on a topic". This could be writing impersonally, too, about, say, ambition and its reverberations into people's lives; those corporate high-fliers of the 1980s, for instance, or those politicians we've known who would be Prime-Minister-at-any-cost.

If you wished to take on the topic more personally, you could reflect on your own ambitions, their nature, and their importance in your life; even your judgement on them. Have they acted to close life in for you, when you'd expected they'd open it out?

Or you could record a reflection on a love relationship, what you offer as well as what you look for; the costs of pledging, as well as the rewards.

The expectation would be that you thus get an overview of your topic for subsequent meditation; see more clearly where *this* is and *that* is, and what is more important than *which.*

The *New Diary* takes all this rather further; for which, go to the chapters themselves.

Finally, for our purposes, the author recommends seven special techniques.

The first is *Lists.* Drawing up lists from which one can take off into extended writing.

Here's one of mine, to hand in a drawer:

Lawn mower
Spain photos
Helen's estate
Dubbo postcards.

This is currently my list of tasks to attend to this week. Hardly promising as a resource, you might think; but one could certainly write a good deal about each.

That lawn and mower have proved something of a desperate saga since we moved into this house a year ago; and surely demonstrate that once the gods have taken a real set on you ... !

The photos of a fortnight wandering Andalusia and Castile already have a few orts-scraps-and-fragments of diary attached, and require only some industry to generate a good deal more. After all, any Mediterranean venture is a gift for a diarist.

Aunt Helen's estate? The problem there would be to come to an end of writing about it! There are several crammed boxes, with each and every item having some specific provenance and association.

As for the Dubbo cards, from friends of a decade back when we were in the area for a time, I could explore heaps of past through these.

This kind of listing mightn't always provide highly dramatic opening for therapy, but it can highlight order and values in your span of years and additionally act as a kind of traffic calmer across life's expressways.

Here's a list from Tristine Rainer:

One diarist wrote the stepping stones of his father's life:

1. **Mother ran away**
2. **Assumption of responsibility for siblings**
3. **Youthful professional success**
4. **Romance and marriage**
5. **Children**
6. **Growing success and rewards**
7. **Disillusionment and the search for meaning**
8. **Attempted escape into charity work**
9. **Failure at attempt to give it all up and start again**
10. **Sickness and dying.**

When the list had completed itself the diarist could understand the relatively minor part he inevitably played in the total context of his father's life. He could feel the movement and integrity of his father's journey as separate from his own.

The experience of Tristine Rainer's diarist is of a significance changing completely when one puts events in the larger perspective.

Most of the Ms Rainer's "Seven Special Techniques" — for example, *Portraits, Guided Imagery* and *Altered Points of View* — have been touched on already either in the earlier chapters of this guide or in what I've reviewed of *New Diary*; but consult the book itself for further suggestions.

Another publication in this area, one that might surprise, is from Alcoholics Anonymous the *Fourth Step Inventory: General Directions.*

This is, of course, directed towards a specific group with a specific disablement, alcohol addiction and its associated problems. As the tract declares, the "drinking problem" will in fact have been generated or at least exacerbated by situations preceding it.

It has been our experience that when we stop drinking, the problems that were actually caused by the drinking will disappear. This leaves us with the problems that caused us to

drink. These as you are perhaps beginning to find out, are the ones that stay painfully with us unless we do something about them.

What is interesting here, is that AA sees as a first line of attack on these preceding problems, *writing them down*!

Buy paper and pen and start writing ... It's the writing it down that helps trigger the release.

The *Fourth-Step Inventory* follows the other publications referred to here in urging that everything be written down, without constraint. It is to be:

... for your eyes only. You are going to tell it to someone but this is FOR YOU. If you decide to erase or scratch something out, DON'T DO IT. It might be one of the keys that would unlock some part of your personality that is hidden from you.

It should include:

......the resentments, fears, guilts, hates and sex hang-ups that you can remember. What you want to be aware of is your REACTION to what happened to you. A moral inventory deals with feelings, both good and bad. Don't get into only what was done TO you (i.e. "I resented my mother because she favoured my sister and didn't love me" or "I hated my father for whipping me in front of my friends"). Don't get only into what you did TO someone: "I used to tell on my brother so I would look good to my parents," or "I felt superior to my brothers and sisters because my parents favoured me," etc. It just goes on and on: "I resented children teasing me about my clothes", or "I was afraid and didn't want to fight" or "I felt guilty about masturbation".

These and their like are seen as "negative feelings about ourselves and others that have wrecked us spiritually, mentally and physically" — through, in this instance, alcohol abuse.

This AA material doesn't, however, lead towards recording any of these matters in continuous narrative form. Rather, the addict seeking release is presented with a list of questions — 151 of them! Several of these are in fact a battery of sub-questions!

Here are the first seven (of forty) childhood questions:

I. What kind of relationship did your mother have with her parents?

2. What kind of relationship did your father have with his parents?

3. Were you wanted at birth? Write out the circumstances of your family at the time of your birth, things such as family size, age differences, financial status.

4. Was there laughter in your family? Arguing? Depression?

5. Were other people living with you?

6. In general, describe what you think your family thought of you.

7. How old were you at the birth of your brothers and/or sisters? How did you feel about the new arrivals?

To work through all these would certainly be to research thoroughly one's self, and provide another point of departure for self-healing autobiographing.

There are also sections and questions on adolescence and adulthood.

For the full text of *Fourth-Step Inventory*, try AA direct.

A final title worth drawing attention to is Ira Progoff's *At A Journal Workshop: the basic text and guide for using the Intensive Journal Process*.

This work outlines many innovative techniques for generating material from inner sources, though some might find themselves not entirely simpatico with the "philosophy" and vocabulary involved. Here's an example:

We begin the work of Time-Stretching by drawing ourselves into an atmosphere of stillness. Our eyes closed, we let ourselves inwardly feel the movement of our life. We try to keep our judgements and our opinions out of the way. Without comment, we simply let the movement of our life present itself to us in whatever forms and divisions it wishes. That is how we get the basic listing of Steppingstones that gives us our framework and starting point.

Our first step is to list the Steppingstones of our life, bringing them together concisely and spontaneously. Our next step is to feed them back into the process of our inner experience. We do this by reading the list as a whole first to ourselves in silence ... so that we can experience the inner continuity that underlies and connects the various changes and cycles of each person's life.... We describe more fully each of the Steppingstones that we have listed. We do this as preparation for the expansive work of opening out the details and contents of the individual Steppingstones periods.

For this next step we return again to silence so that the process of life-recollection will be carried out in a deepened atmosphere of stillness. ... With our attention directed to a particular Steppingstone Period, we let memories come to us. These will be recollections of our past experiences, and they will also be recognitions of intersections in our life.

I conclude this chapter with a red light of warning.

It will be self-evident that in order to deal constructively with the deeper and more significant of our experiences, psychotherapy is engaging with potent and atavistic forces that have potential for explosive outcomes. Even if I were a trained psychotherapist, I'd be handling patients somewhat as an electrician handles a live cable!

Those of you who have had experience with so-called addictive personalities, for example, will be all too familiar with the baffling unpredictabilities one encounters. To say nothing of conflicting theories of treatment — as, Supportive vs Confrontationist.

Even Virginia Woolf, with all her patently successful writing out of tensions and torments in diary, fiction and letters, could topple back into overwhelming despair. Here is the letter she left for her husband Leonard before she drowned herself in the River Avon:

Dearest, I feel certain that I am going mad again: I feel we cant go through another of those terrible times. And I shant recover this time. I begin to hear voices, and cant concentrate. So I am doing what seems the best thing to do. You have given me the greatest possible happiness. You have been in every way all that anyone could be. I dont think two

people could have been happier till this dreadful disease came. I cant fight it any longer, I know I am spoiling your life, that without me you could work. And you will I know. You see I cant even write this properly. I cant read. What I want to say is that I owe all the happiness in my life to you. You have been entirely patient with me and incredibly good. I want to say that — everybody knows it. If anybody could have saved me it would have been you. Everything has gone from me but the certainty of your goodness. I can't go on spoiling your life any longer.

I don't think two people could have been happier than we have been.

You will understand, then, why I believe that those setting up as gurus in this field should possess, above all else, a profound humility towards their authority and their skills. Indeed, it has been aptly stated that many gurus are made into gurus only by the needs of those in need!

It bothers, too, that some authors in this self-healing field instruct readers to do this-that-and-the-other to recover, stabilise or enrich their lives, but offer little persuasive evidence as to whether the bases on which their theories stand are sound or whether the methods outlined do work.

One should discount testimonies from folk that such-and-such a procedure worked for them. It might have done so, of course; but one event following another doesn't necessarily mean that the first produced the second. You need not fear going to bed on the grounds that more people have died there than anywhere else.

Remind yourself that many disorders are self-limiting. Heaps of patients would recover anyway, without treatment. At times, even in spite of it! So it's not only in earlier centuries that mountebanks set up platforms and preached snake oil to the unwary and credulous.

Hence, take advantage of the treatments and support offering — but with caution.

Finally, there's the direction in which self-exploration propels — *inwards*!

How easy it is to become obsessively preoccupied with this self that is you! This isn't at all to assert that self-scrutiny and self-knowledge are unimportant or undesirable. Quite the contrary: each is vital to our understanding of our nature and of our limits.

There is another direction in which one can also journey — outwards.

Records abound of those who've found identity and spiritual satisfaction and peace-with-self through service to others. In generous and supportive friendships and in free contribution to family (tho' *not* as general dogsbody!) and to community and to ideals.

I know of no guidebook suggesting you throw away your diary for a time, with its inescapable absorption in self, and instead head out into that battered old world of pain and loss and poverty and confusion and solitariness and addiction and roll up sleeves and actually lose that self to find it; as the Gospels, at certain points, exhort.

Camille Paglia, that somewhat renegade feminist, declared perceptively that to be perfectly free (of obligation and commitment) is to die by earth, air, fire and water; which seems about as comprehensively as one *can* die!

I suggest then that the whole point of any expedition towards self isn't just to arrive and settle — mission accomplished — journey's end — finito!

Self, as destination, should not be regarded as a terminus; but rather as a launch pad into living, a point for fresh embarkation into life.

Particularly if you finish your self-discovery and self-healing with the bonus of a swag of additional autobiographical material.

Chapter Eight

L'Envoi

What's L'ENVOI?

It is an epilogue, or discourse to make plain
Some obscure precedence that hath tofore been sain.
[William Shakespeare *Love's Labours Lost*]

Actually the pages that follow are not simply to make plain preceding obscurities. Indeed, I would hope that obscurity in this text features only through its absence!

Nevertheless, there is a sense in which this short section will catch up, and act as appendix to, much that has been implicitly referred to in earlier chapters, but was passed by in the more general sweep and rush.

For example: if you are looking to submit your autobiography to a commercial publisher, there are certain mechanical matters to take into account. Some of these apply too if you intend to run off more than just a handful of copies and to circulate these fairly widely.

For a start, use reasonable quality A4 paper — one side only — numbered, with good margins and double spacing.

Add a "title page", giving your name and address, the title of your work and the approximate number of words.

Always keep a mastercopy! Post in a strong envelope. Include return postage, preferably an SAE.

I have been berated by editors both for including a covering letter and for not doing so. Probably it's best to allow the work to announce itself unless there is some pertinent matter you think the publisher would want to know — as a centenary, or some unique access your work offers to a group (jazz) or period (The Depression) or fashion (Gentrifying the Slums). Mention any specific qualifications that are relevent to your writing, too, (e.g., forty years a ship's captain or vineyard owner).

What is important in this area of submission, though, is that you choose a suitable publisher in the first place.

If the House specialises in medical texts or astrological publications, the reader won't look beyond your title page, unless, say, you've been a clairvoyant — which you would point out in an accompanying letter. (I can't think of any conceivable reason a publisher of medical texts might consider an autobiography — not even from an author of medical texts!)

The other publishing option is what is known, somewhat ambiguously, as self-publishing. There are two sub-options here: the first is vanity presses. These advertise in *Writer* magazines and literary journals and sometimes in the Yellow Pages of phone directories. For a fee, they will, they claim, edit, publish and sometimes distribute your work.

This fee is usually hefty; and according to report, the editing and distribution often not satisfactory and sometimes virtually non-existent.

Unless I had some very good recommendation, I'd stay away.

The second option ranges from just some printing equipment in a small office, mainly producing business cards and simple leaflets, to the full publisher who will as a side-line put out your book for you, but on contract, not as an enterprise of his/her own. Editing and distribution might be negotiable too.

In the midst of this range are firms that specialise in small runs of books for authors like, probably, most of the readers here (see Appendix). Such firms will quote you for, say, fifty copies of 128 pages. (Usually, the more copies, the cheaper per copy. But don't get carried away and end up with a storage problem!) Artwork and the like can be included. Present day technologies can give quite an attractive product.

Many such firms have good reputations, but tread warily nonetheless. Ask to see examples of works like yours. Perhaps even contact other client-authors. Make very clear that you want yours to be like *that* one.

If you are really keen and impatient to get something of your life into print, you could try writing small sections of it for magazines, newspaper supplements, even radio talks. *Bread and Dripping Days*, for example; or *My Vietnam-Protest Phase.*

You would expect to be "selling" only First Serial or Radio Rights with such material, so it can be used subsequently for your book. It would be courtesy to tell any publisher of such earlier publication; indeed, it would enhance your prospects for getting an attentive reading.

"Top" journals do publish such short autobiographical pieces, but even more do many of the "little" magazines, right down to club quarterlies and in-house annuals and district news sheets and office rags and trade journals. Indeed, many editors are eager for such copy.

(A woman once asked me whether I knew any place where she could sell evangelical Greeting Card verse! I *was* able to find somewhere: in New York!)

Do keep records of where you submit your manuscript, plus the dates of submission and (Oh dear!) return. Also, keep track of costs of postages, stationery, depreciations on typewriter/WP, phone calls and transport costs related to the project, as if you do make any dollars from sales then these expenses incurred become legitimate deductions for taxation purposes.

In Chapter Four, *Getting It Together,* I did not posit any best-length for chapters, though some writer guides do suggest 2,000 words.

I have found it better to let each chapter have its length determined by the topic's area; but probably best not over 4,000 words.

Here, for example, the sections on *Family History* and *Self-Healing* are relatively quite long; but it seemed artificial and disruptive of flow to break them up.

Some first-time writers, particularly older generations, fret a great deal about grammar and spelling and other such formal elements; and writer guides often have sections on punctuation and the like.

It is true that "correct English" gives a good impression and saves the publisher editing time and expense; and so gives your work a good start. It is equally true that intelligent punctuating is important for meaning, as:

Bill said Tom is dead.

"Bill," said Tom, "is dead."

The punctuation here is literally a matter of life and death!

I do not think, though, that you can transform "bad grammar" into "good grammar" just by learning some rules. While such can clarify and systematise, a "feeling" for good prose comes considerably from reading and writing.

In any case, if your autobiography is compelling enough, the House will employ somebody to tidy up the writing.

The notion of "correct" spelling is a newfangled one. In the Eighteenth Century (when the most elegant English ever, probably, was being written) one spelled how it sounded; and if others understood, the spelling was acceptable. Even today, a language like Italian is largely phonetic — you spell it as it sounds.

Unfortunately, spelling has since become linked with literacy and social class; so it is prudent to avoid "errors" in your script. Dictionaries will help; but some words, you need to know how to spell them before you can look them up! Hence if your spelling offends, get some "good speller" to vet your final version for you. Most WP packages have a "spell-check" facility.

I have assumed throughout this guide that central to your purpose is to write up your life *as it was*. Hence I've not followed other guides which suggest that you (say) fabricate to give appropriate atmosphere to an incident; or make characters larger-than-life to engage readers; or for any other such readability "saleability" purposes, distort the history.

Titles

The title of your work might simply be your name together with some indication that the work is autobiography.

Elinor Burrows: A Life

The Life of James Britten

Additionally, your title could offer some item suggesting your life's frame or character, as you-as-autobiographer see it.

Benjamin Lascelles, Master Mariner

***Our Kate: An Autobiography* (Catherine Cookson, Corgi 1974)**

Finally, your book could use a title much like that of a novel or play or film, one which prefigures themes as well as catching the eye. Such titles are frequently quotations, so if you look for one thus it would be worthwhile browsing through *The Oxford Book of Quotations*, a *Shakespeare Concordance* or the like.

***Cracking Nature's Mould,* The autobiography of a scientist (King Lear, SHAKESPEARE)**

***Present Mirth*, The autobiography of a television comic (Twelfth Night, SHAKESPEARE)**

***One Musketeer,* A lighthearted account of life in the armed services. (The Three Musketeers, ALEXANDER DUMAS)**

***Into the Whirlwind,* The persecution and death in Stalinist Russia. Eugenia Ginzburg, Collins/Harvill, 1967)**

Take a moment to glance through the titles in the Bibliography at the back of this volume. These exemplify the range of possibilities.

It will be self-evident, of course, that the most demanding part of writing an autobiography is not the choosing of the title!

Endings

My strong preference is for brevity — just a paragraph or two. This need not be any old farewell, though. It could integrate with and possibly echo the themes and trajectory of your volume. This would give a pleasing roundedness to your work; a sense of symmetry, of satisfying conclusiveness

Here is an example of an ending. Check back to p.16 and note how closely it catches up its opening.

I sit now, at that same desk of my father's where I commenced this inscription of my life — though on this occasion there are no garden trees nor any great silver ocean to look on. It is night, and the study curtains are drawn.

You will understand, if you have followed to the end of these pages, why I am both wealthy ... and alone. Mammon has proved a predatory god; and to Mammon I have sacrificed my frail Jenny, my two sturdy children, troops of friends. Only material assets remain to share my solitariness; or those relationships which cash can purchase, but which are not worth the dust the rude wind blows.

So it will be now, to the end. Yet if I could only have back those misdirected days. Trade all that wealth ... for love, human warmth, service to others.

But those years now? *Ubi sunt*? [AUTHOR'S EXAMPLE]

Two other examples of openings relating to endings.

Kingsley Martin was a minor literary figure of the mid-twentieth century, perhaps best known for his long editorship of the Leftish journal *New Statesman And Nation*. The second volume of his autobiography, *Editor*, was published by Hutchison in 1968. Here is its opening:

I came to London in the autumn of 1930 to seek my fortune. In this book I want to record something of the mental climate in which I found myself immersed and to describe its problems, as they appeared to me at the time. Many books are published about the thirties, but they seem concerned to mainly show how feeble, absurd and misguided we all were. These are the characteristics attributed by each generation to their parents' generation. I want rather to show why we failed, and, above all, to explain our struggles to prevent the Second World War.

Here is the conclusion:

Looking backward and forward today, I think we were right in the thirties in believing that the future of mankind depends on morality, personal, political and international.

Very few of our new, scientific supermen seem today much concerned with the everyday issues of poverty, social misery and the threat of another world war. Einstein indeed said that the men of science have slipped so much that they have come to regard "servitude to governments as their natural lot". Half a century earlier another great scientist, Thomas Huxley ... said that "the prostitution of the mind, the soddening of the conscience, the dwarfing of mankind are the worst calamities." We shall not solve these problems by flying to the Moon.

Finally, Charles Hamilton is a different figure altogether, with the distinction of having published probably more words in English than any other fiction writer in the history of the universe! Sixty million have been estimated, though further works, under further pen-names, occasionally come to light.

He wrote "Boys' Stories"; and his most famed character was Billy Bunter, the fat school boy at Greyfriars. For better or for worse (given the gender stereotyping and ingrained class assumptions) several generations of young Empire males, and not a few females too, were reared on this fiction and its clones.

Hamilton's autobiography is disappointing — little depth, little intimacy. This eccentric and very private author even writes it in the third person, under his best known pen-name, Frank Richards. The conclusion and opening, though, feature that symmetry we've been observing.

The opening:

Frank Richards, at seventeen, was at a loose end. He was in the perplexing state of not knowing what he was going to do.

So he was, by a curious coincidence, at seventy! But let us not, as the novelists say, anticipate.

What Frank was going to do, and to become, was in those days a problem to which a solution had to be found.

Frank was rather good at chess problems: but not at that sort of problem.

He had many ideas — perhaps too many. He wanted to be either an author or a pen-and-ink artist: or both. He had had, from earliest boyhood, a strong desire to go to sea. He had an almost equally strong desire to become a famous

cricketer. But chiefly, all the time, he wanted to write. And in fact he did write, though his earliest works, dating from the age of seven, are fortunately lost to humanity.

But though he was never quite himself without a pen in his hand, he hardly dared dream of print.

But he had to do something ...

And the conclusion?

Frank is still here. He is still alive and clicking! He is as busy, once more, as in pre-war days. He enjoys writing as much as ever he did: his interest flags no more in 1950 than it did when he wrote his first story in 1890. He passed the seventy mark in the War time. His eightieth birthday looms on the horizon. He envisages it with equanimity.

He will never see Alps or Apennines again. He will never ride on the Corniche road, or sail a boat on Lago Maggiore, or saunter on a sunny boulevard — or even walk up Fleet Street. And he doesn't mind very much. He still finds the world a jolly old place to live in, and is happy and contented. He has many readers, and judging by their kind letters they are all his friends. Every morning he reads "fan" letters over breakfast: which, if it were needed, would put him into a cheerful mood for the day. And when he looks up from the typewriter, at his window over the sea, at the bookshelves with innumerable photographs of young people pinned along the edges, at Sammy the cat watching him solemnly from the cushion in the armchair, he feels he is as lucky in age as he was in youth.

And so, dear reader, adieu!

Well — having so confidently instructed my "dear reader" about bringing his/her volume to a satisfactory ending, it remains now to see whether I can do this with mine!

I have tried over these pages to outline and instance those procedures and skills that make it possible to transfer to paper the life you have experienced; which written record, in its turn, communicates to others something of the substance and colour of that life.

Beyond this exercise in documenting, recreating and communicating, though, has been the implicit assumption that the writing of autobiography is itself part, and a greatly rewarding part, of the life experience. That there is intrinsic value in bringing all your past to life on paper.

Human beings seem to differ from all other creatures in that they live each moment many times over — once as it occurs; and then, at will, in retrospect. So writing your autobiography is not simply reviewing your life; it is also, in a sense, re-entering it. The losses and the griefs, too, as well as the joys and triumphs; because shadows are also and necessarily part of the complete life, the fulfilled life. That nineteenth century Sun Dial that proclaimed:

Horas non numero nisi serenas

[I count only the sunny hours]

had it quite wrong. If all the year were playing holidays/to sport would be as tedious as to work — as Prince Hal noted.

I will allow a Roman poet, Horace, the final words here: he sums up succinctly and with characteristic ease, the purported statement of my own ending:

Omne tulit punctum qui miscuit utile dulci, Lectorem delectando pariterque monendo.

(He has gained every point who has mixed practicality with pleasure, by delighting the reader at the same time as instructing him.)

Does that pass?

Bibliography

Alcoholics Anonymous *The Fourth Inventory*

Cary, Joyce *To be a Pilgrim*

Church, Richard *Over the Bridge*

Crisp, Quentin *The Naked Civil Servant*

Dickens, Charles *Dombey and Son*

Dickinson, Emily *Collected Poems*

Donne, John "The Triple Foole" *Collected Poems*

Facey, Albert *A Fortunate Life*

Forster, Ken *Dornford Yates* in *Postmarks, Places & People*

Goodman, Lord *Tell Them I'm On My Way*

Gray, Nancy *Compiling Your Family History*

Gunn, Mrs Aeneas *We Of The Never Never*

Hamilton, Charles *The Autobiography of Frank Richards*

Heald, Bernard *Time's Winged Chariot*

Herriot, James *All Creatures Great and Small*

Horace, Roman poet, 65-8 BC

Lee, Laurie *I Can't Stay Long*

Lee-Scarlett, Errol *Roots and Branches: Ancestry For Australians*

Martin, Kingsley *Editor*

Masters, John *The Road Past Mandalay: A Personal Narrative* and *Bugles and Tigers*

Moon, Kenneth, et al, eds. *A Surry Hills Childhood*

Moon, Kenneth *Hawkesbury's Black Horse Inn*

Morgan, Sally *My Place*

Paglia, Camille *Sexual Personae*

Pope, Alexander "Epistle to Dr Arbuthnot" and "An Essay on Criticism" *Complete Works*

Progoff, Ira *A Journal Workshop*: *The Basic Text and Guide for Using the Intensive Journal Process*

Puritan Diaries Sundry Sources

Rainer, Tristine *The New Diary: How to Use a Journal for Self-Guidance and Expanded Creativity*

Sand, George *Histoire de ma Vie*

Schweitzer, Albert *My Life and Thought: An Autobiography*

Sellar and Yeatman *Ten Sixty-Six and All That*

Shakespeare, William *Hamlet* and *Love's Labours Lost*

Steinem, Gloria *Revolution From Within: A Book of Self-Esteem*

Sterne, Laurence *Tristram Shandy*

Thomas, Dylan "Fern Hill" *Complete Works*

Woolf, Virginia *Diaries* (5 vols); *Letters* (6 vols); *A Sketch of the Past* in *Moments of Being*; *To The Lighthouse*

APPENDIX

Self-Publishing

Below are details of two companies in Australia which will publish your autobiography for you.

Fast Books is the short-run printing system established by book publishers, Wild & Woolley, located in Glebe, NSW.

Fast Books provides a quick turn-around for printing and binding of books in small quantities (50 to 500 copies). It knows all about publishing and can help the self-publisher with cover design, applying for an ISBN and sending books to libraries — as required by the Copyright Act — and for listing in Books in Print. You can also get advice on text layout and typesetting, ink paper and binding.

For more information contact, Fast Books:
16, Darghan Street, Glebe NSW 2037 Ph: (02) 692 0166.

Tryfoss, based in South Australia, offers a similar service and can be contacted on (08) 264 6435. They are also happy to offer a typesetting service and help with layout and design.

You can write to them for more information at PO Box 47, Para Hills, South Australia 5096.